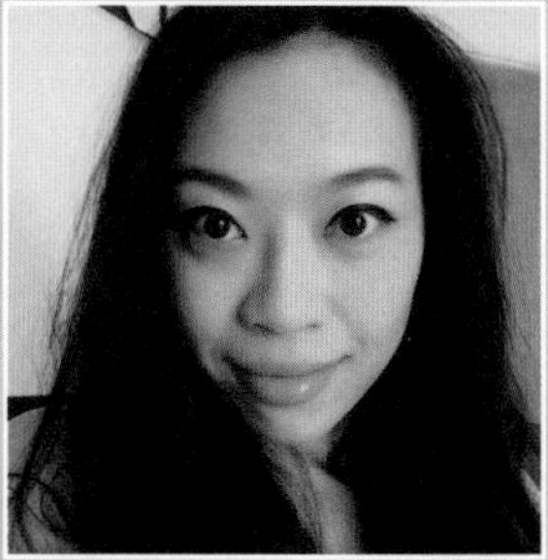

YISHAN LI is an internationally renowned professional comic and manga artist based in Shanghai. A best-selling author, she has sold over 250,000 copies of her books worldwide. Yishan has been drawing manga since 1998 when she was in high school.

Visit her website: www.liyishan.com

Other books by Yishan Li:

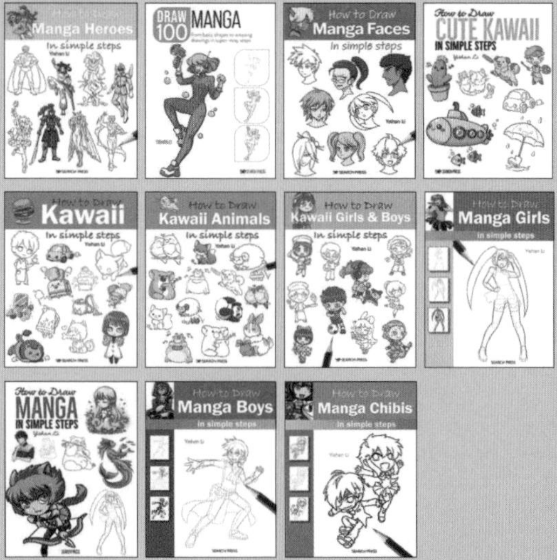
How to Draw Manga Heroes in simple steps
Draw 100 Manga
How to Draw Manga Faces in simple steps
How to Draw Cute Kawaii in Simple Steps
How to Draw Kawaii in simple steps
How to Draw Kawaii Animals in simple steps
How to Draw Kawaii Girls & Boys in simple steps
How to Draw Manga Girls in simple steps
How to Draw Manga in Simple Steps
How to Draw Manga Boys in simple steps
How to Draw Manga Chibis in simple steps

Also in the Draw 30 Series:

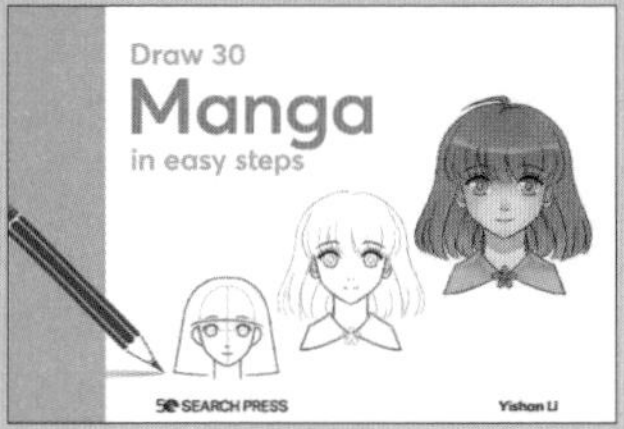
Draw 30
Manga
in easy steps
SEARCH PRESS
Yishan Li

Draw 30
Kawaii
in easy steps

Yishan Li

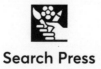

Search Press

About this book

Each of these 30 kawaii drawings has eight simple steps: the first shape is drawn in blue, then new shapes are added in pink. Black lines are used for the final drawing, then the completed image is fully coloured.

Just grab some paper (normal copy paper will do), a pencil (preferably 2B) and an eraser. To finish your drawings you might want to use a black waterproof gel pen, along with whatever colouring method you like!

The most important thing I hope you will learn from this book is to be creative. Everything can be kawaii if you add just a bit of creativity!

Yishan x

The contents

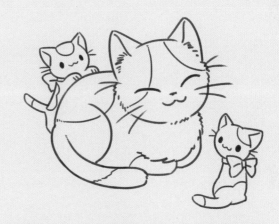

The Drawings

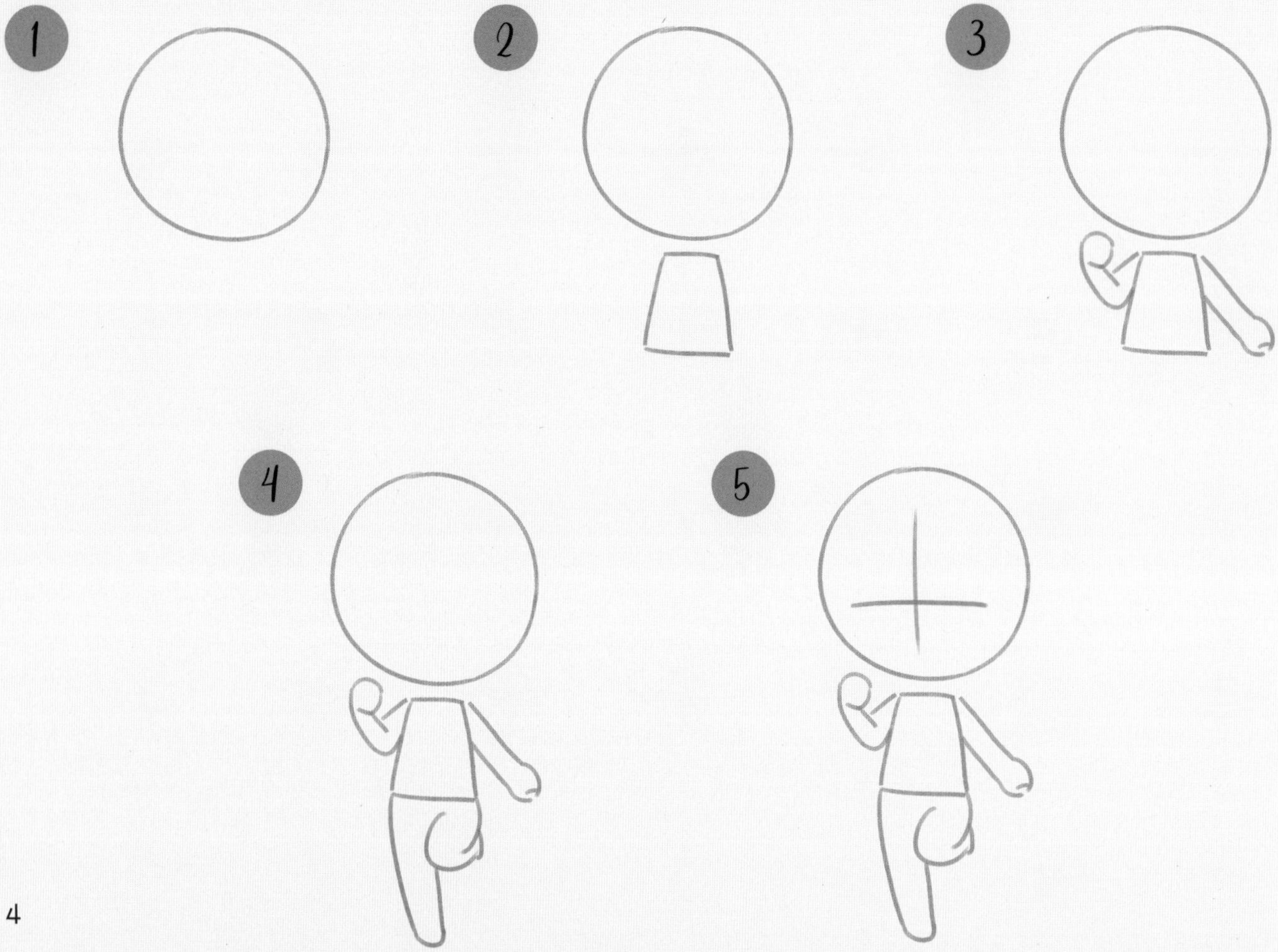
1
2
3
4
5

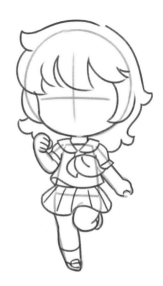

6

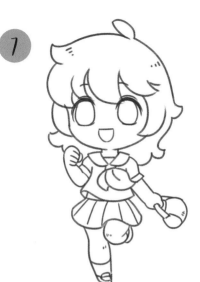

7

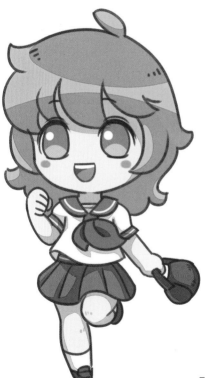

1

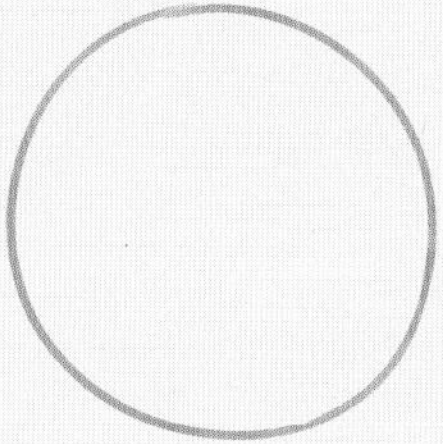

2

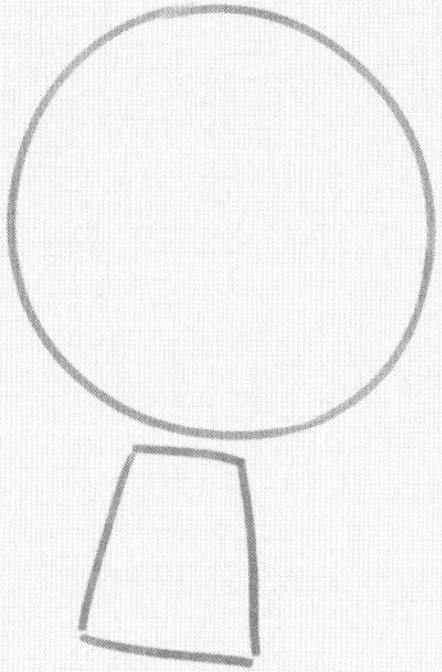

3

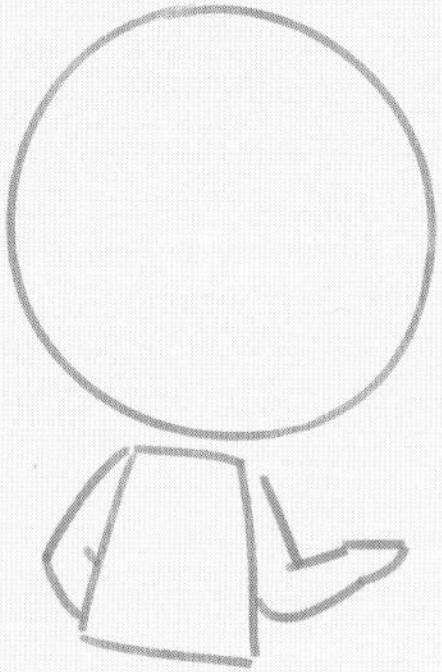

4

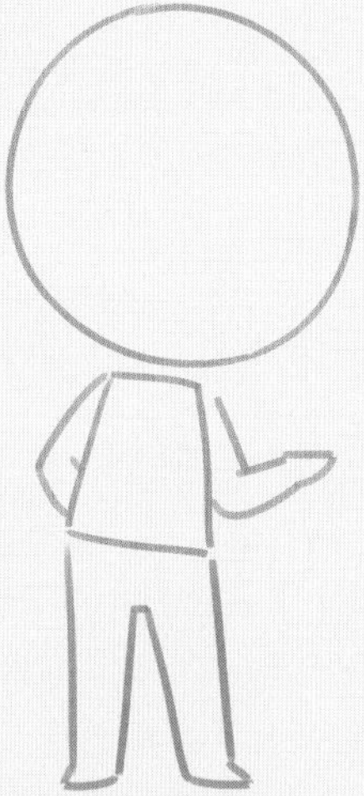

5

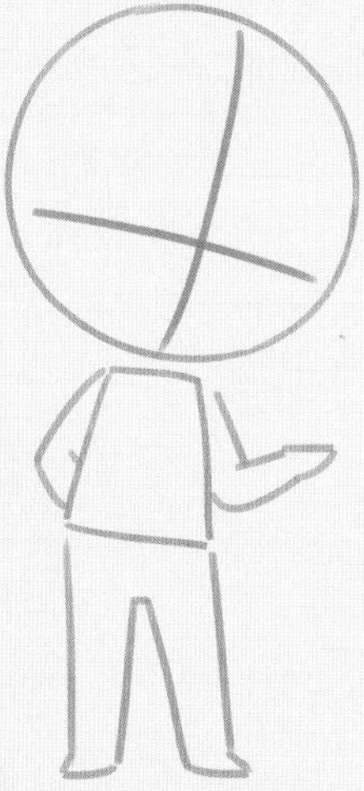

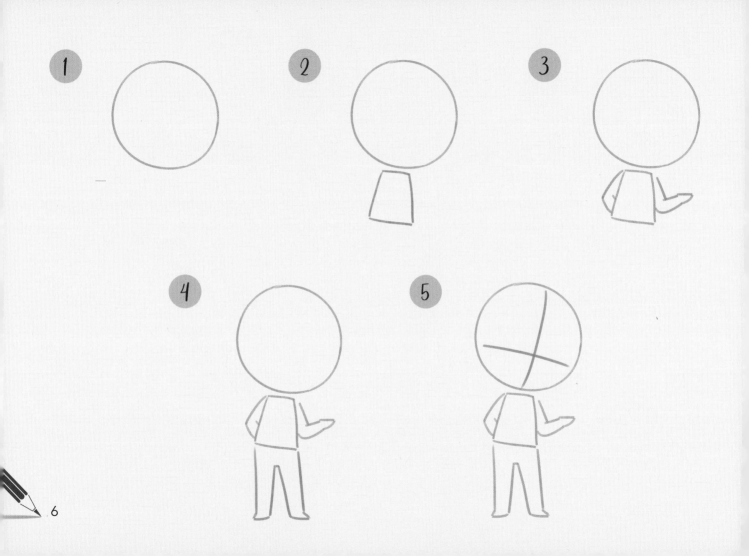

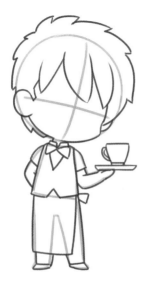

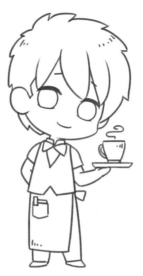

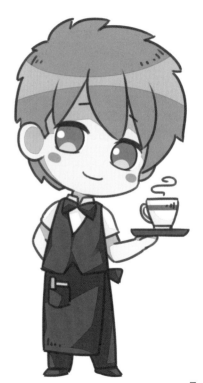

7

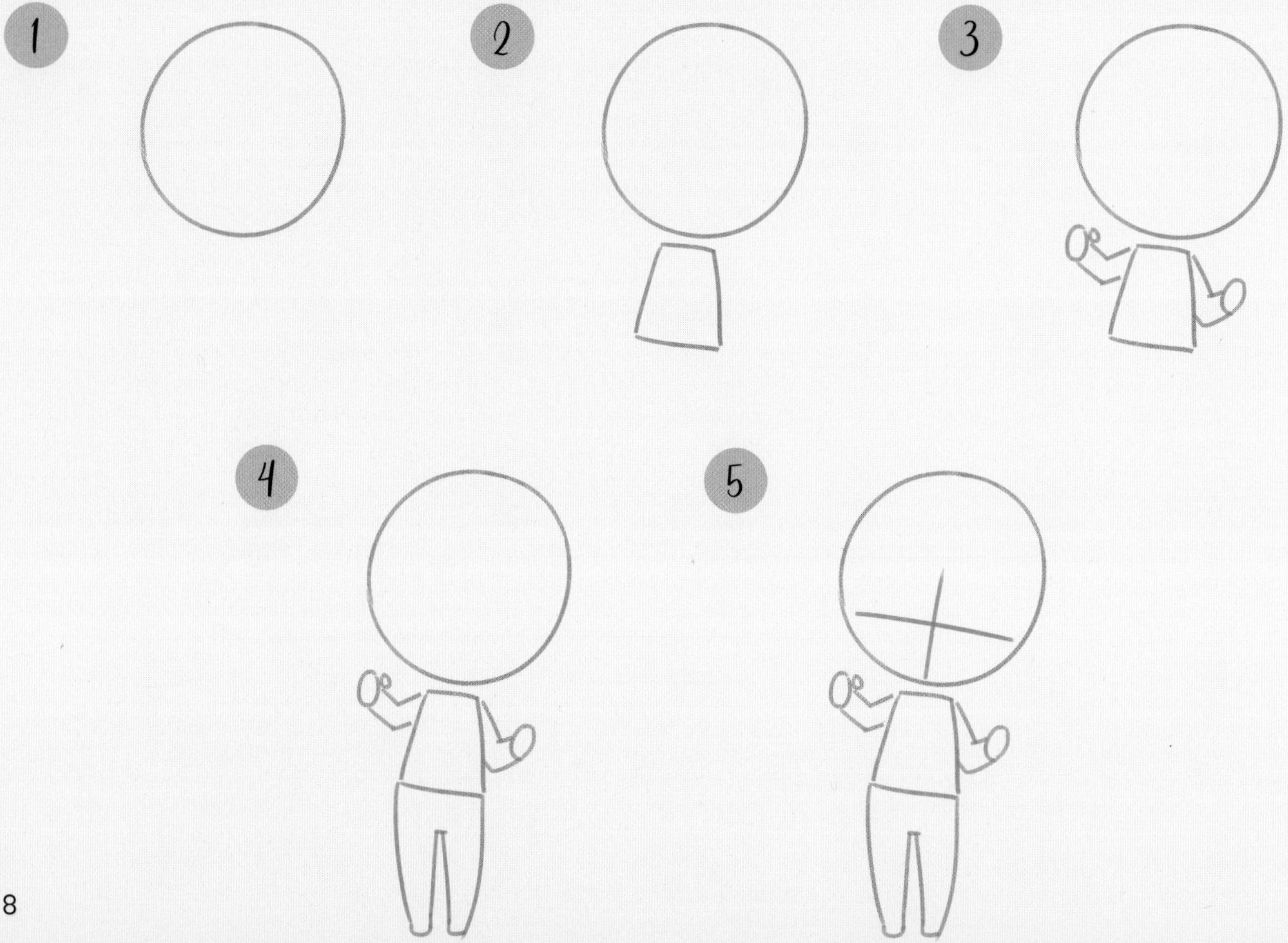
1
2
3
4
5

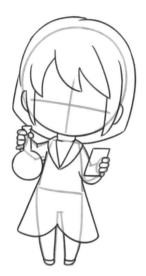

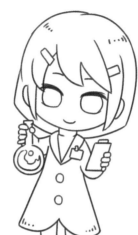

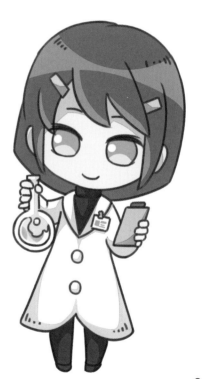

9

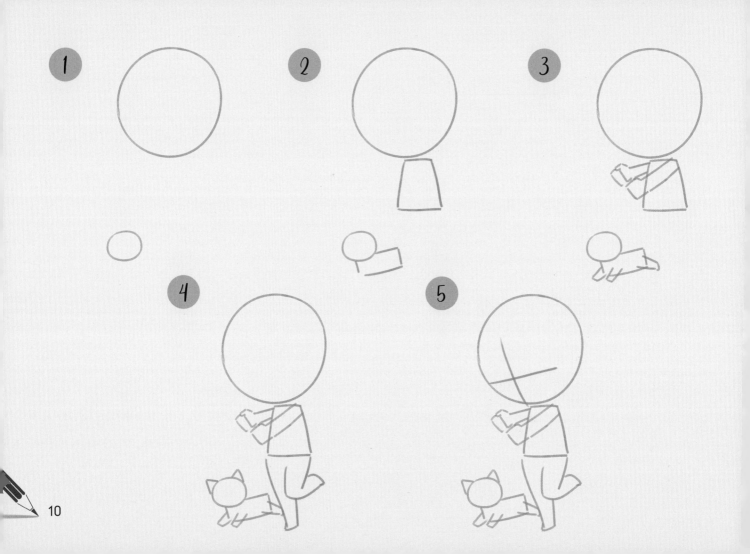

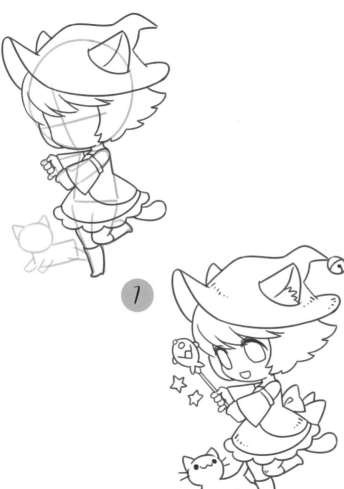

7

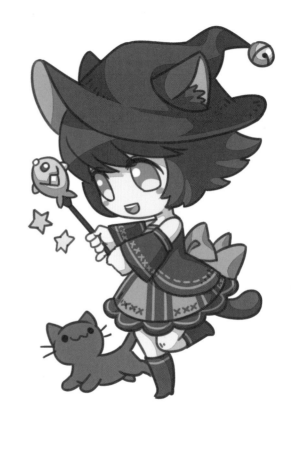

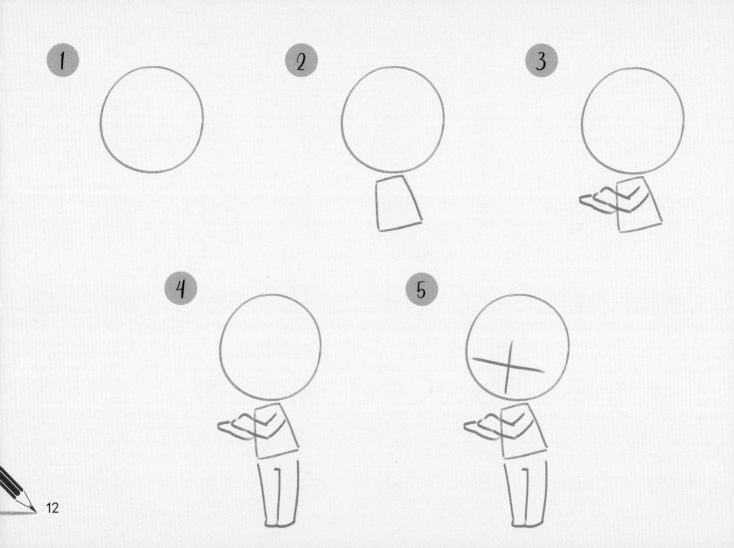

6

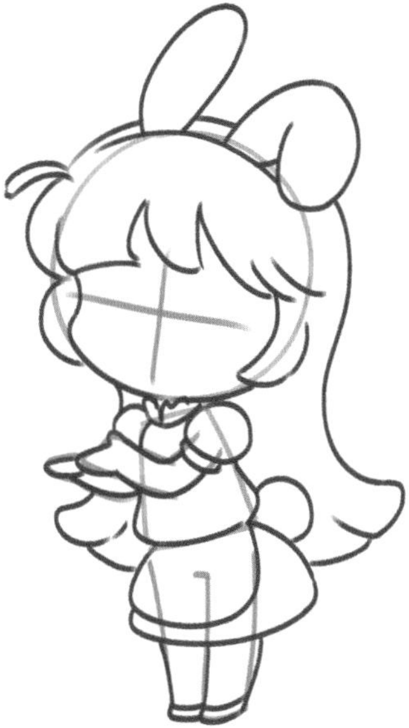

7

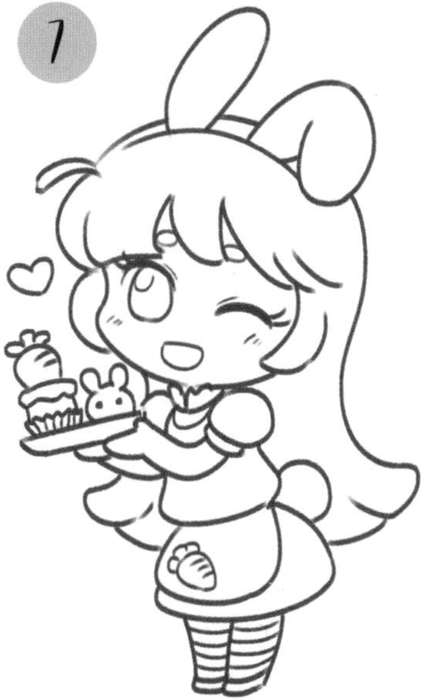

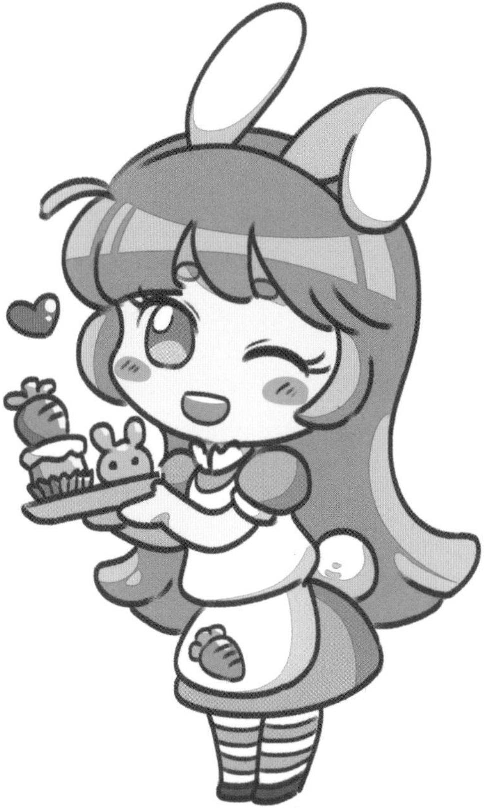

1

2

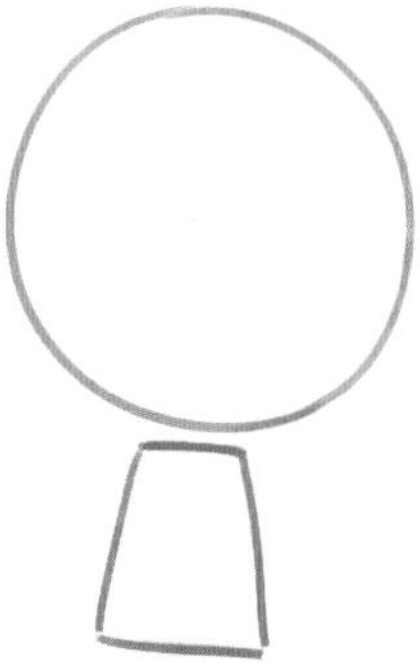

3

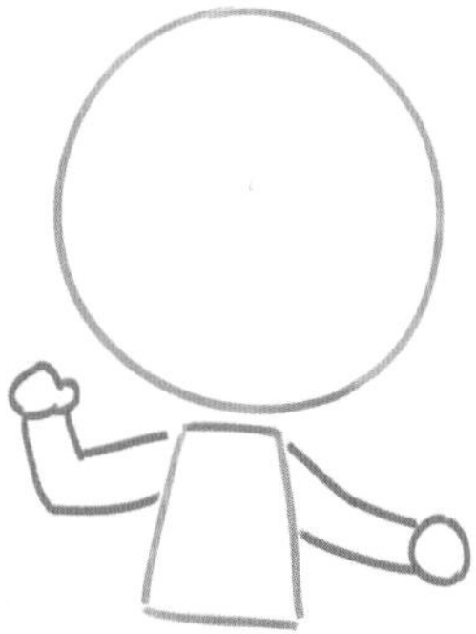

4

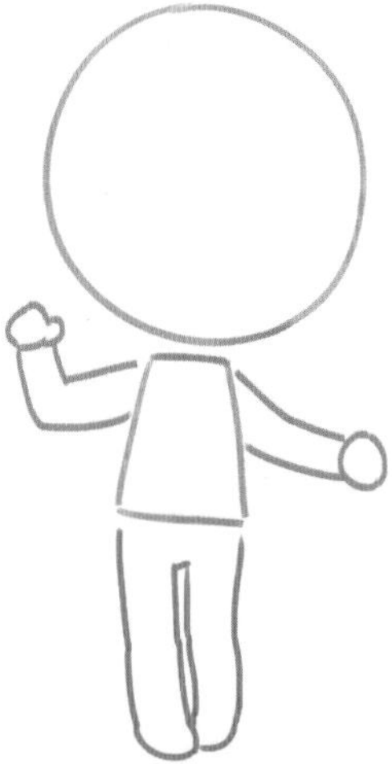

5

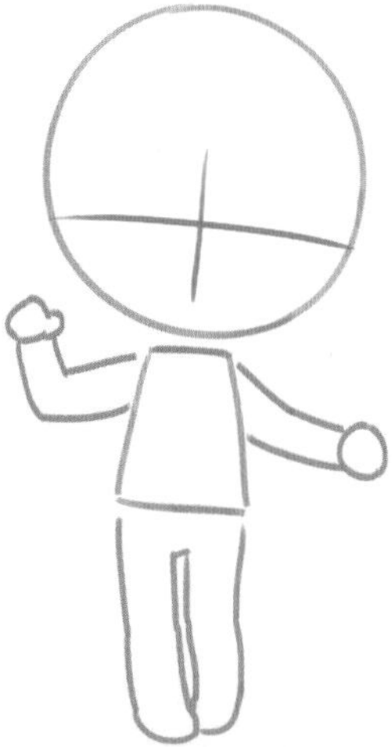

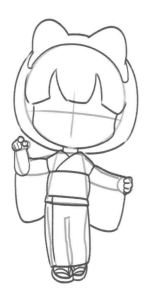

6

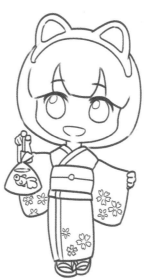

7

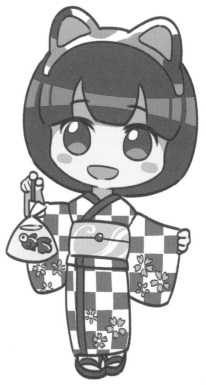

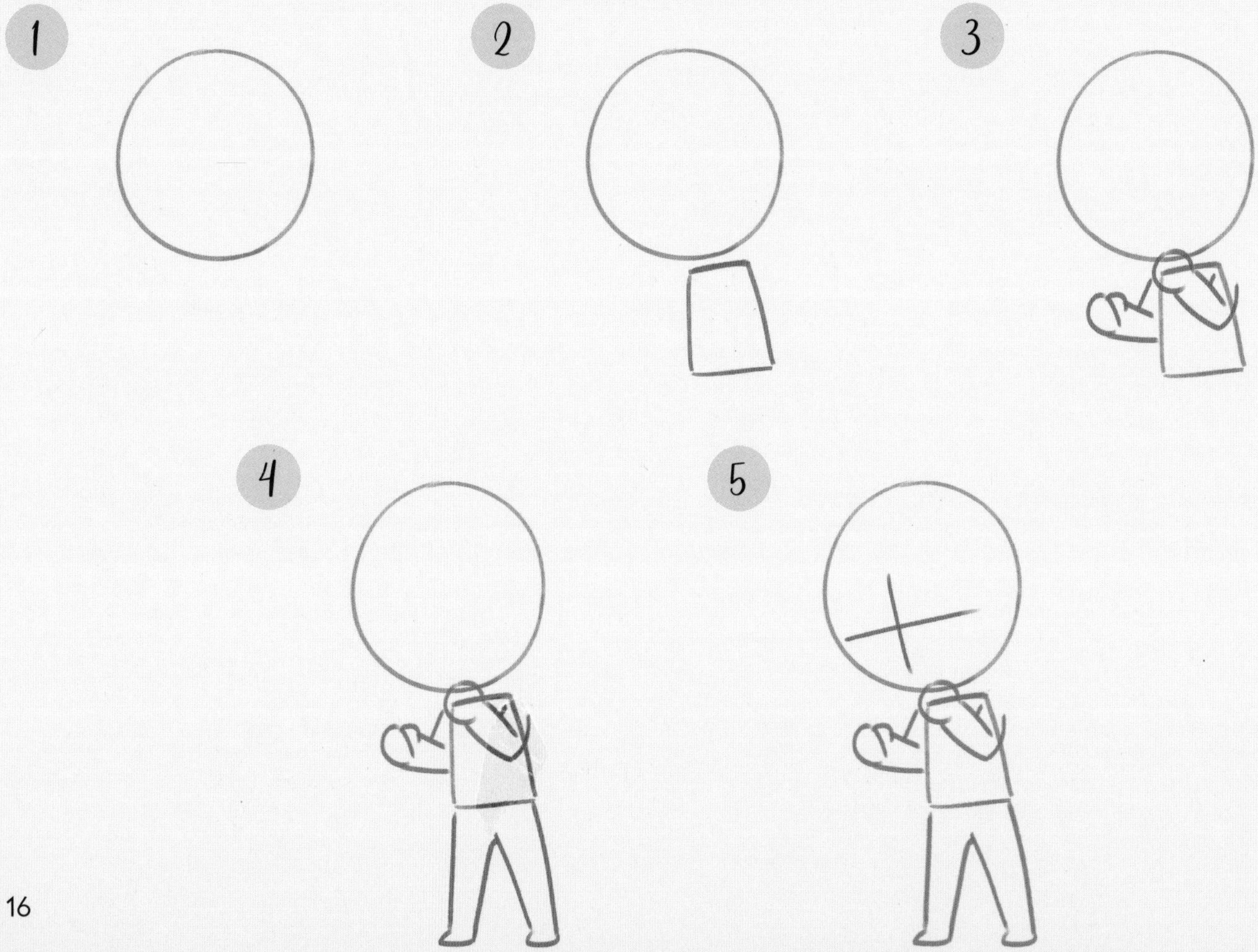
1
2
3
4
5

6

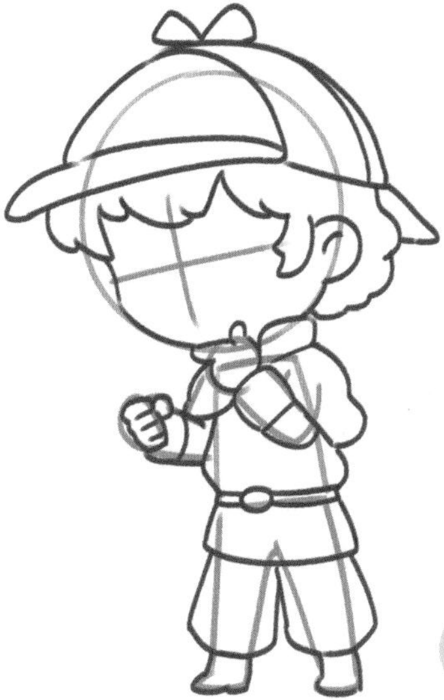

7

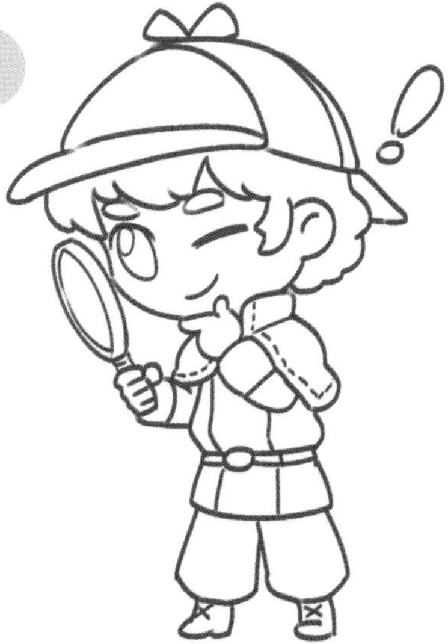

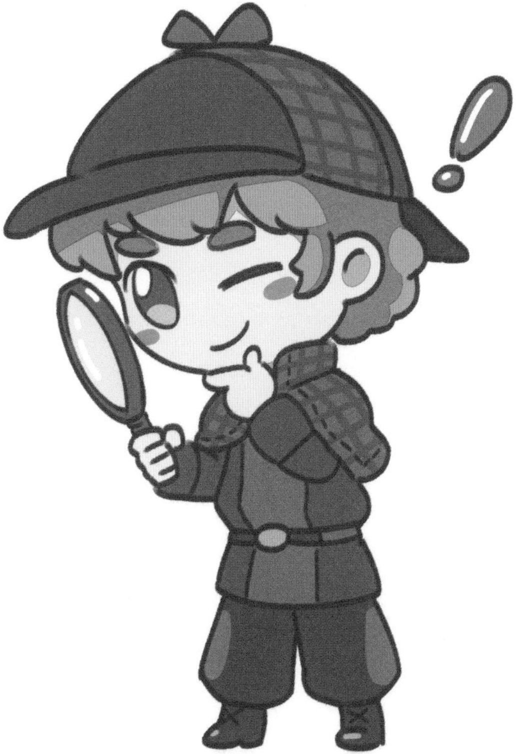

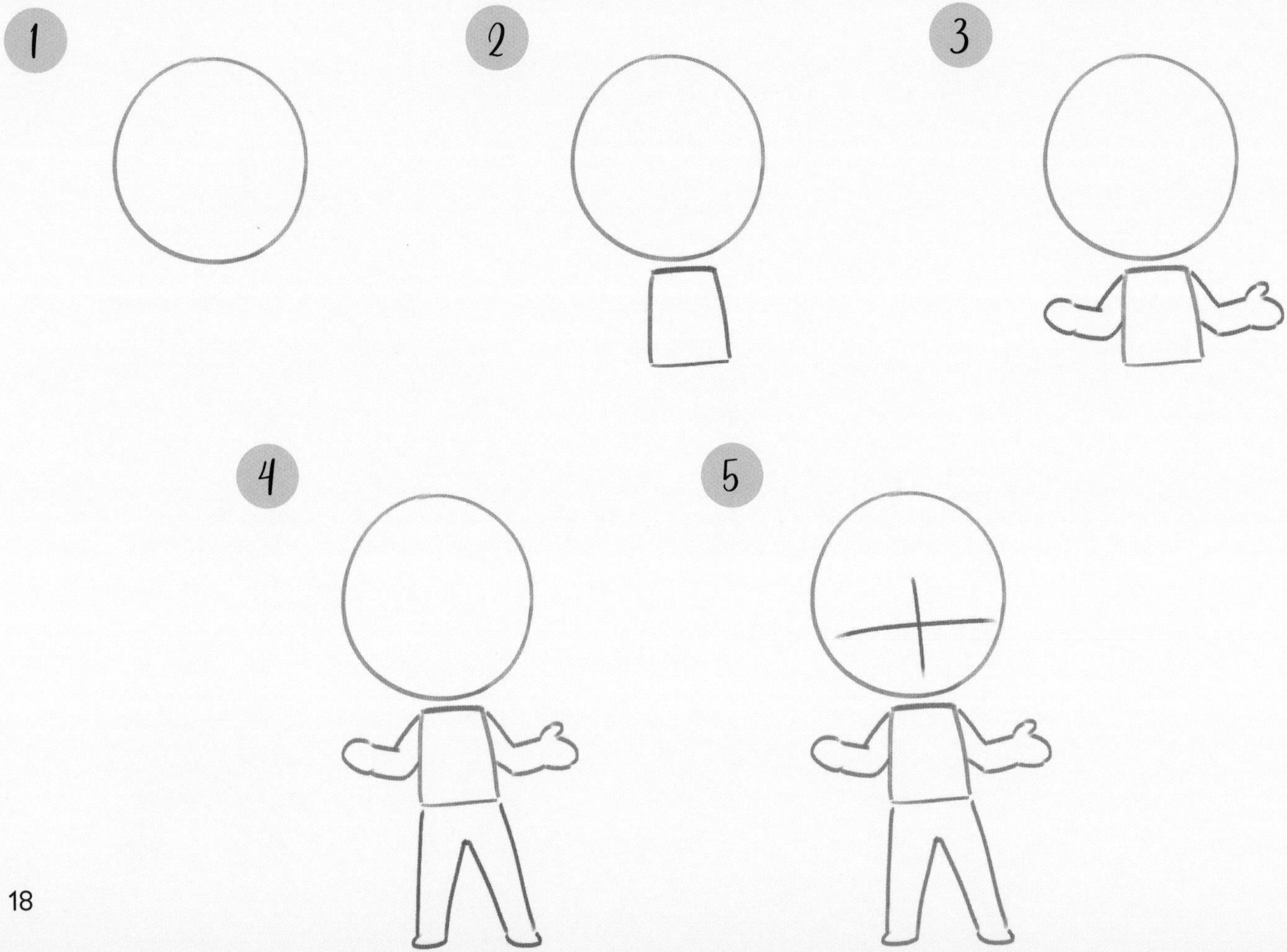
1
2
3
4
5

6

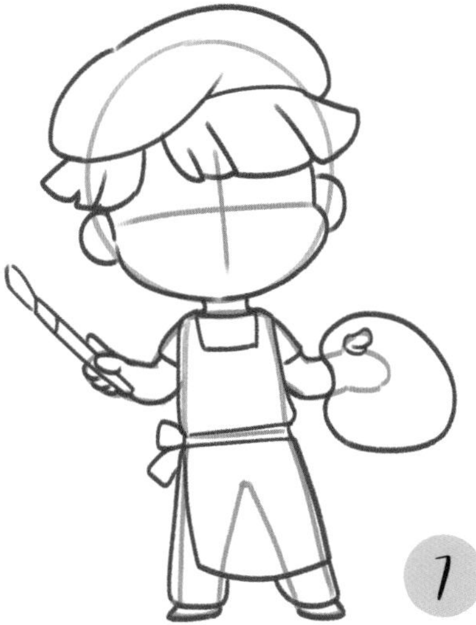

7

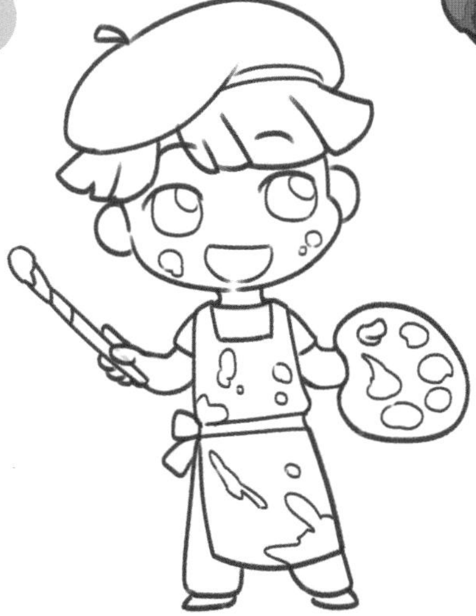

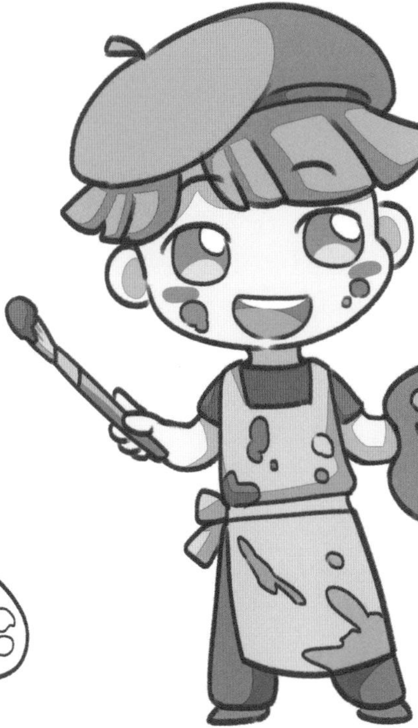

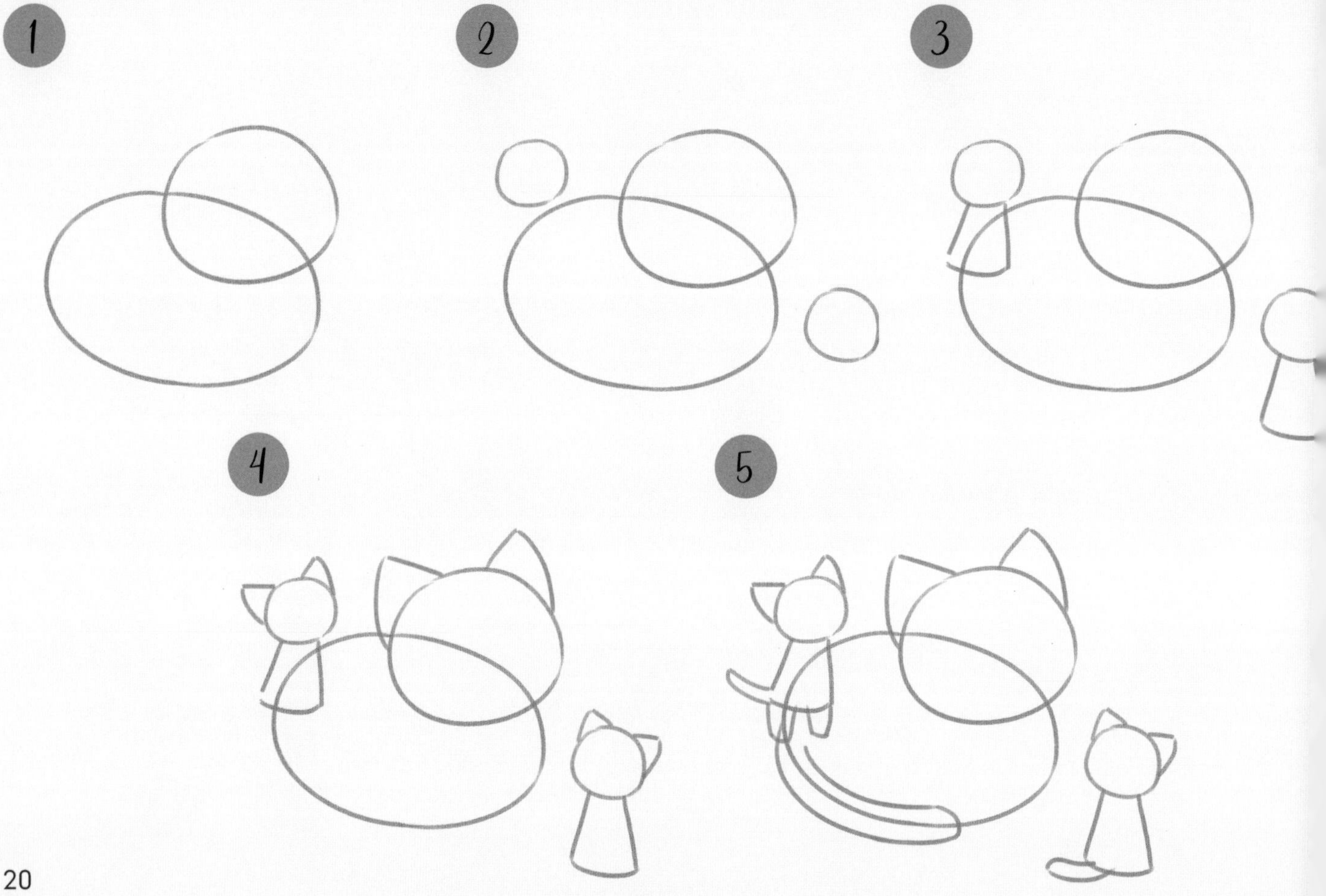
1
2
3
4
5

6

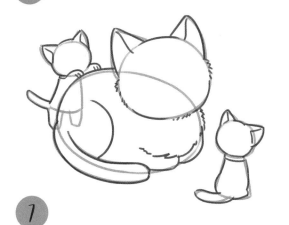

7

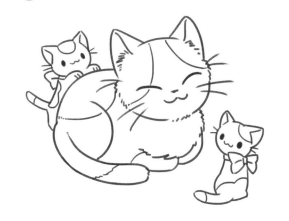

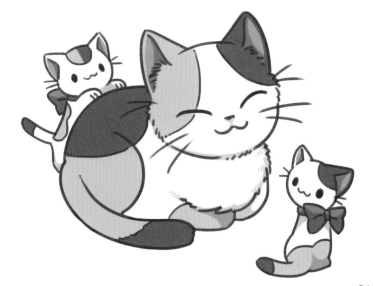

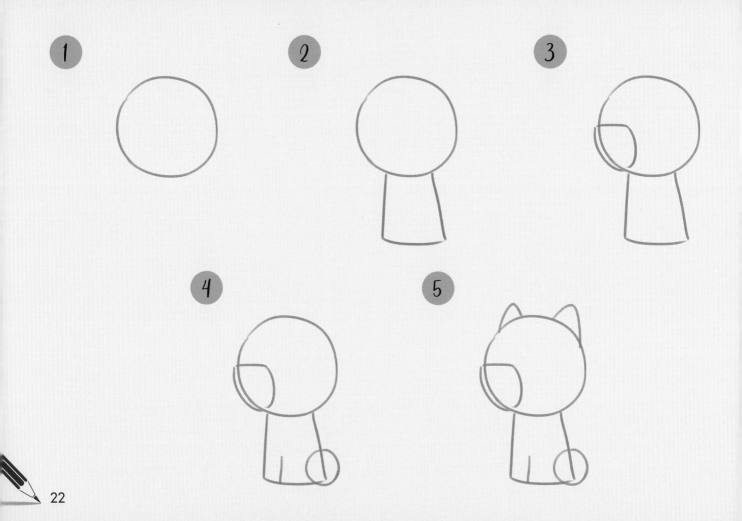

6

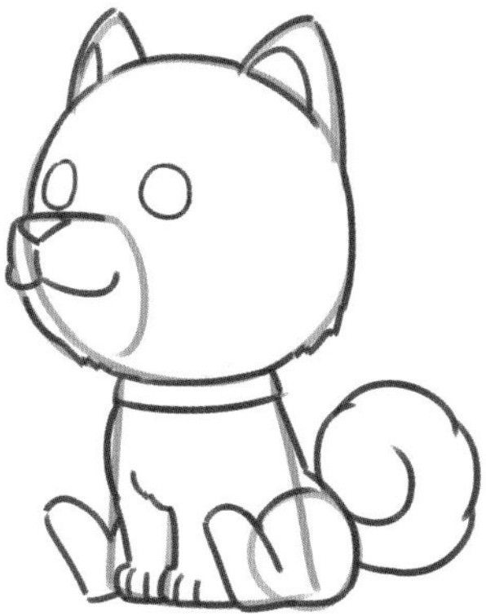

7

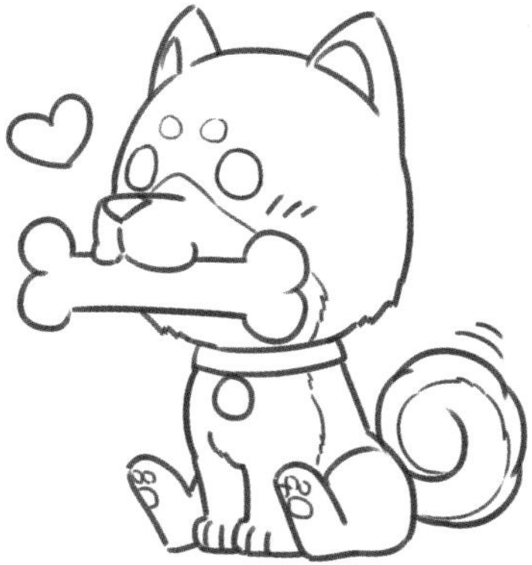

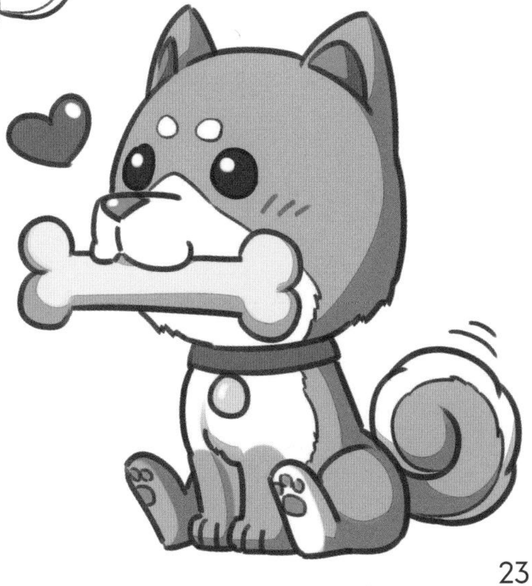

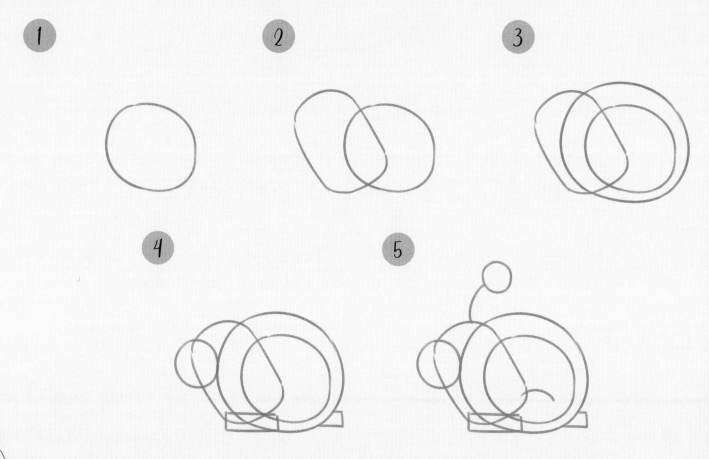

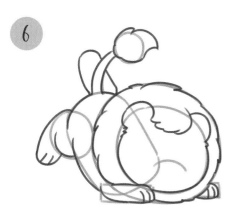

6

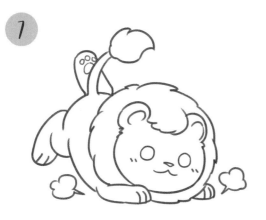

7

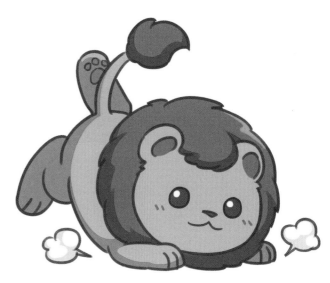

25

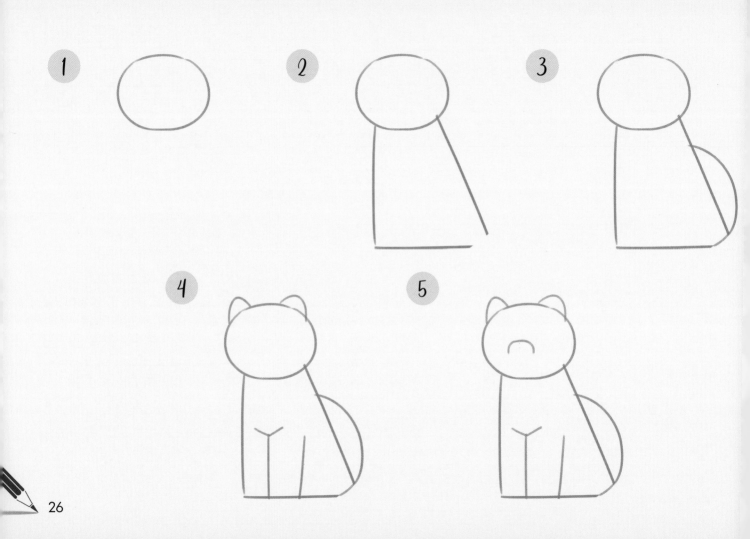

6

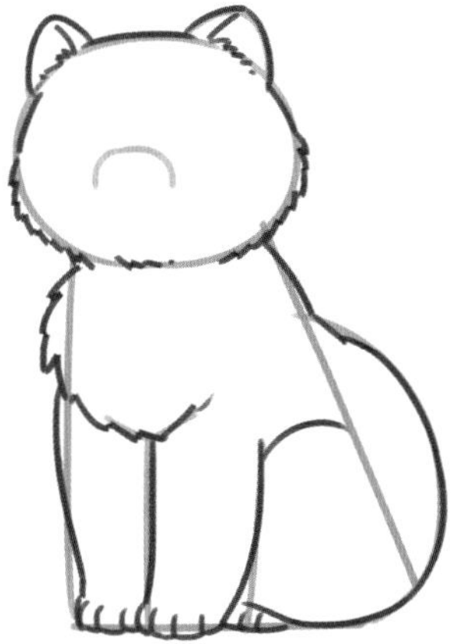

7

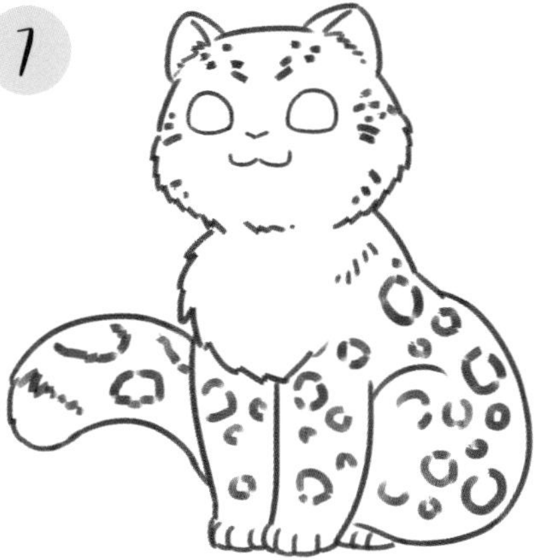

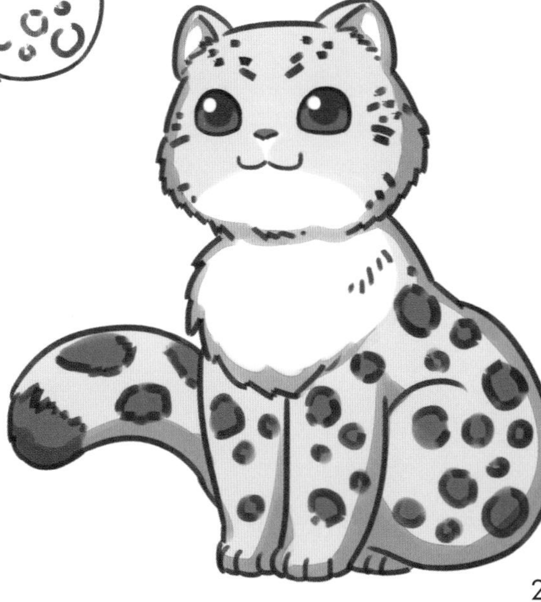

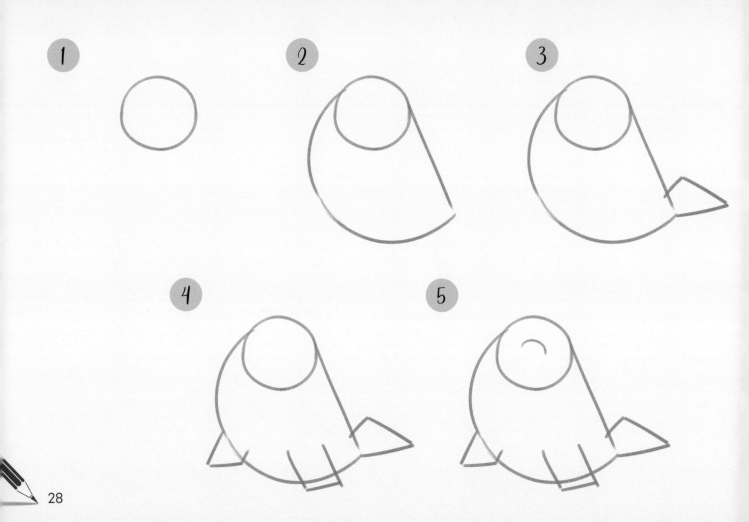

28

6

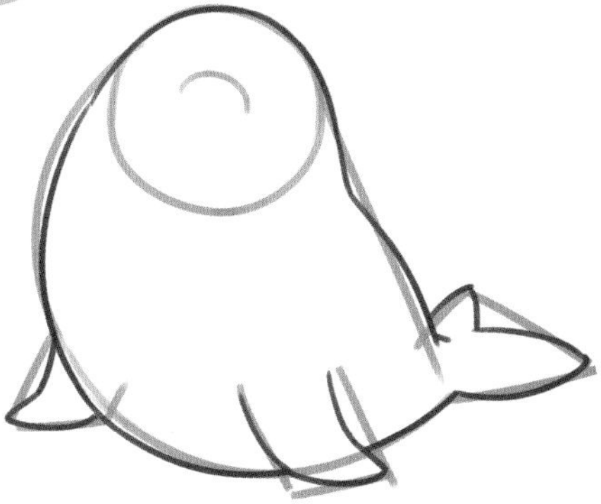

7

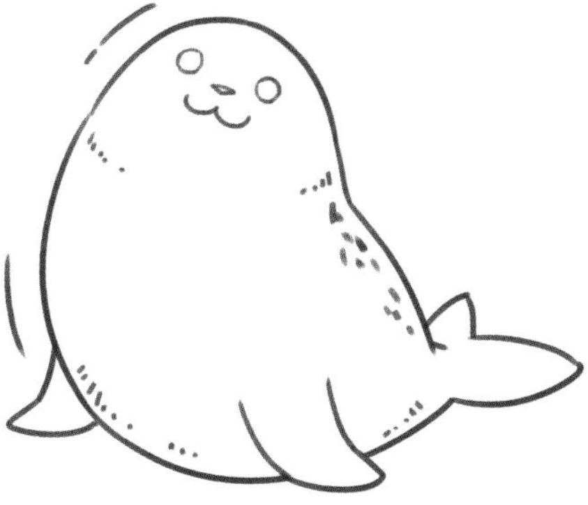

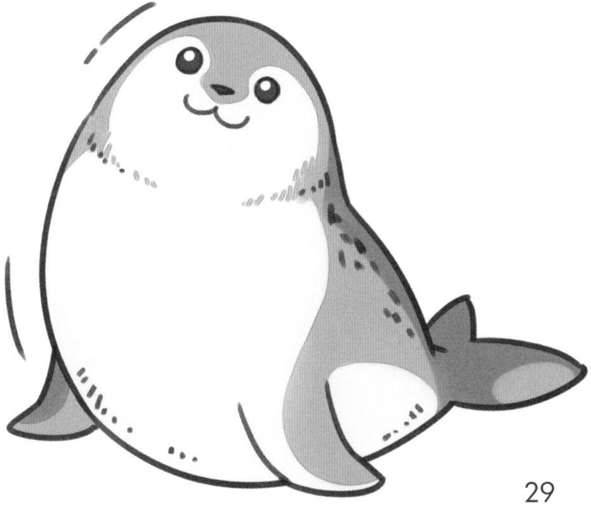

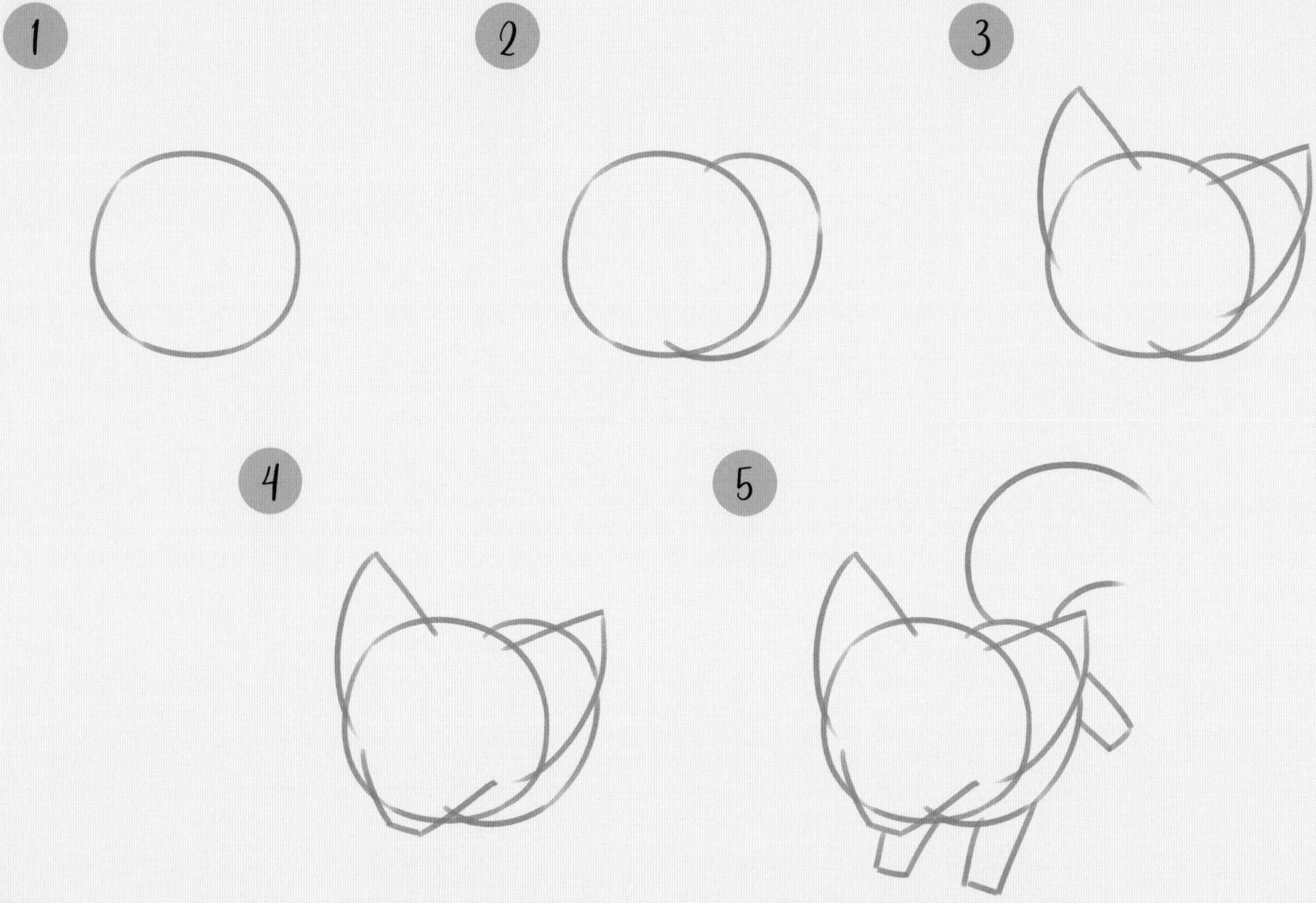
1
2
3
4
5

6

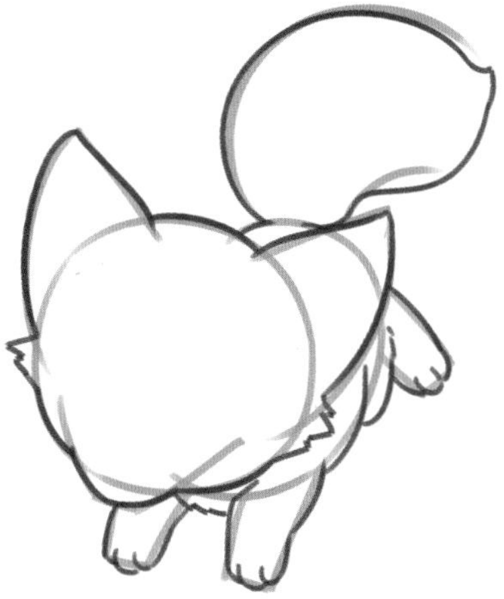

7

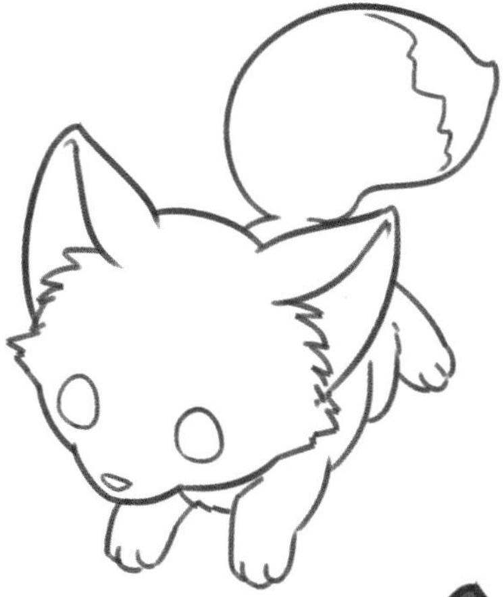

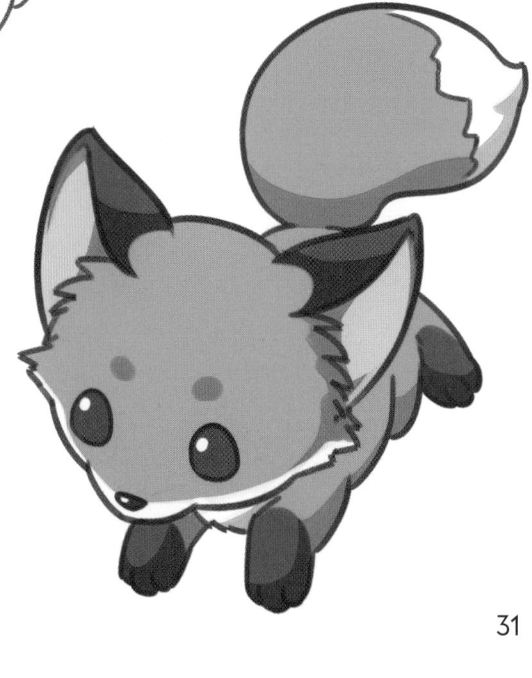

1

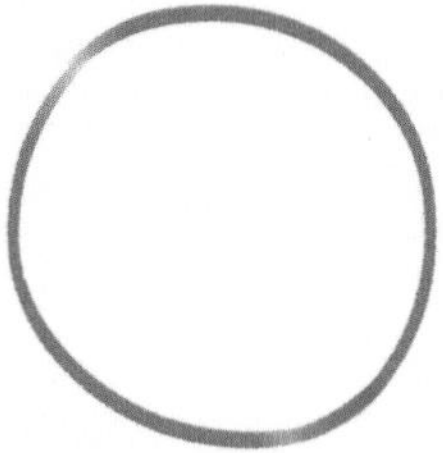

2

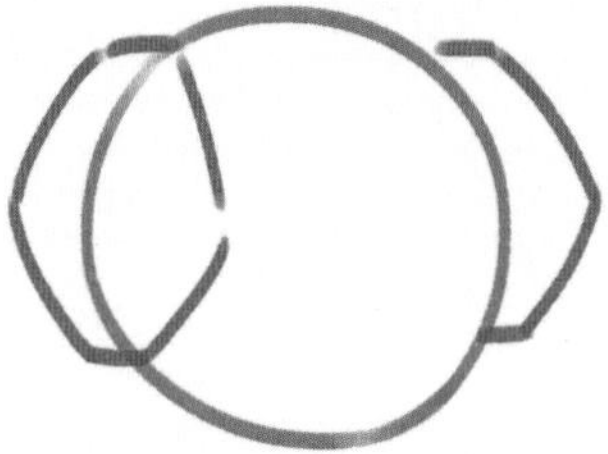

3

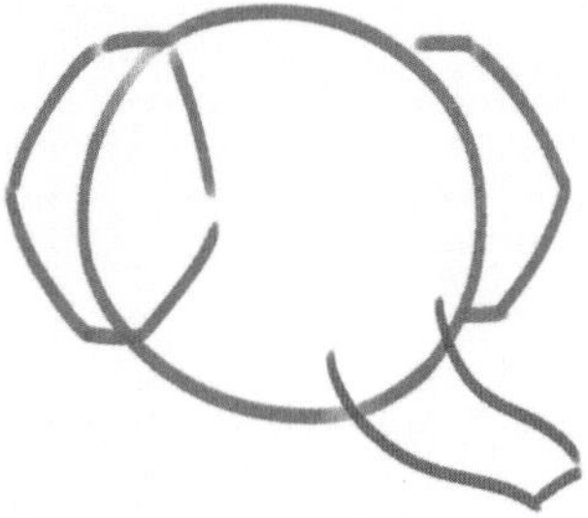

4

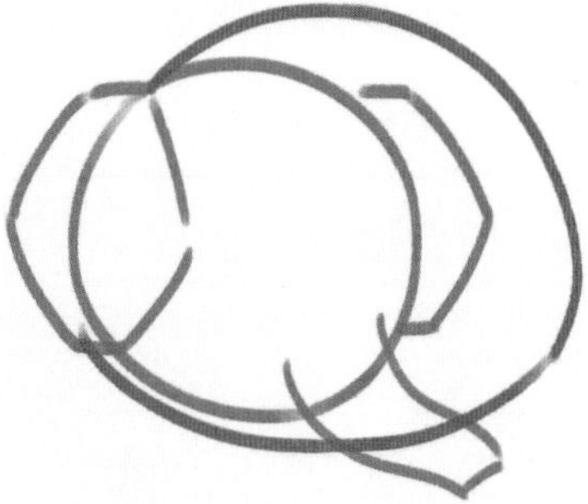

5

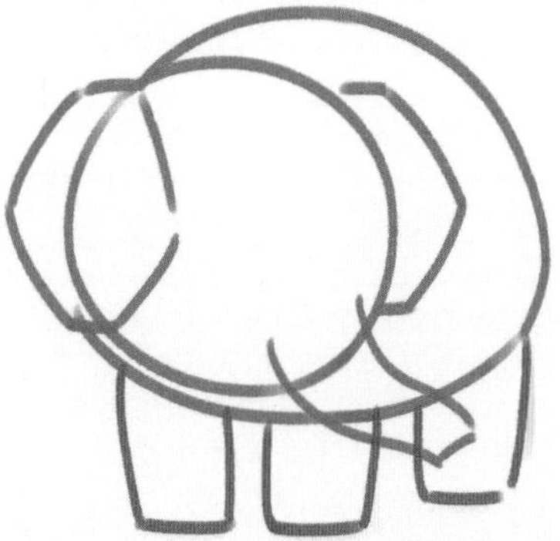

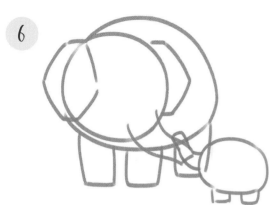

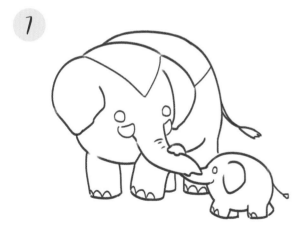

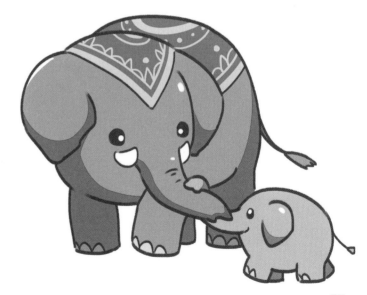

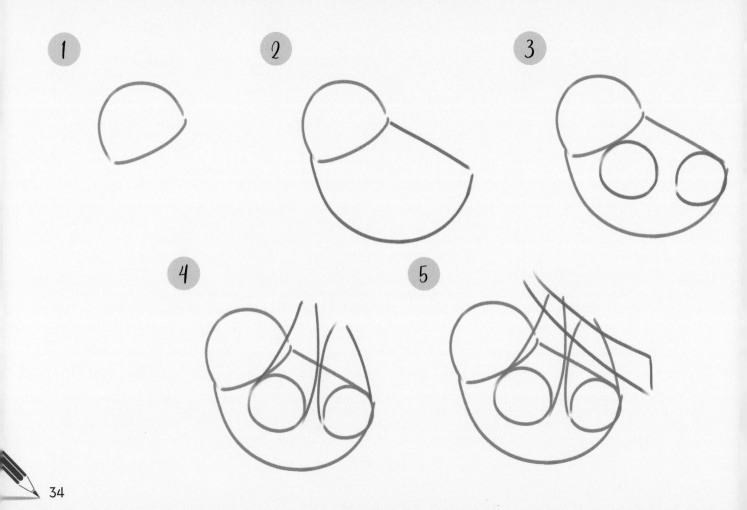

6

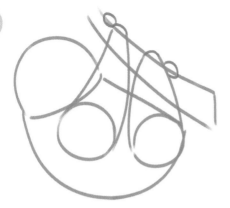

7

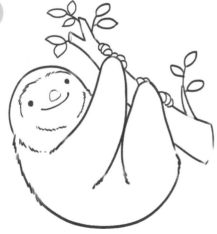

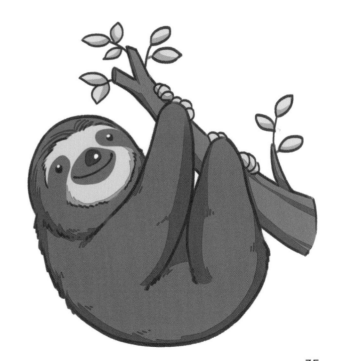

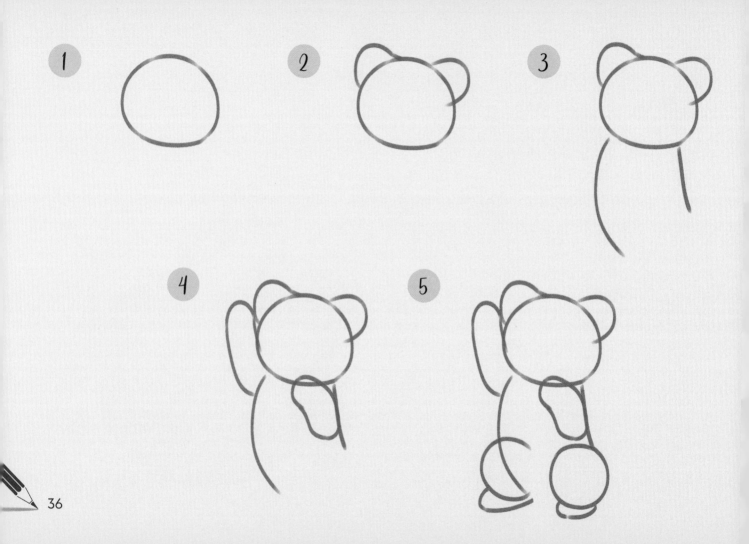

6

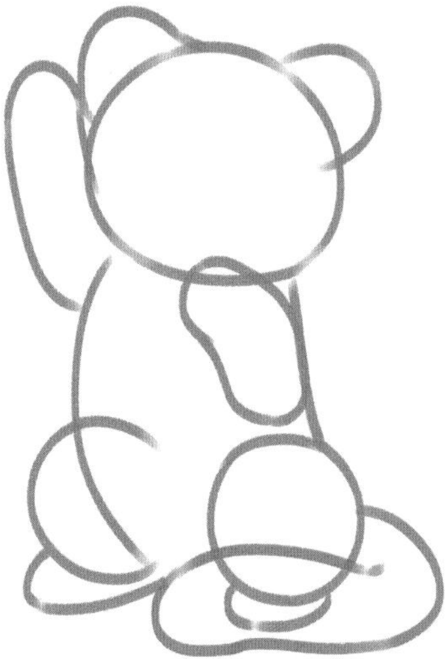

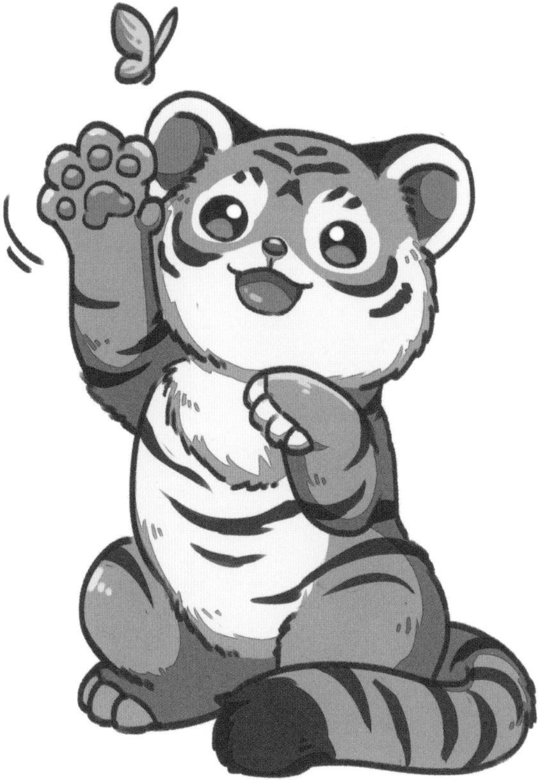

7

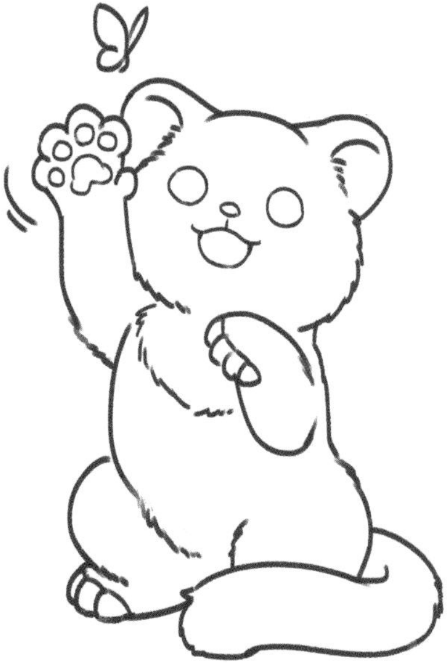

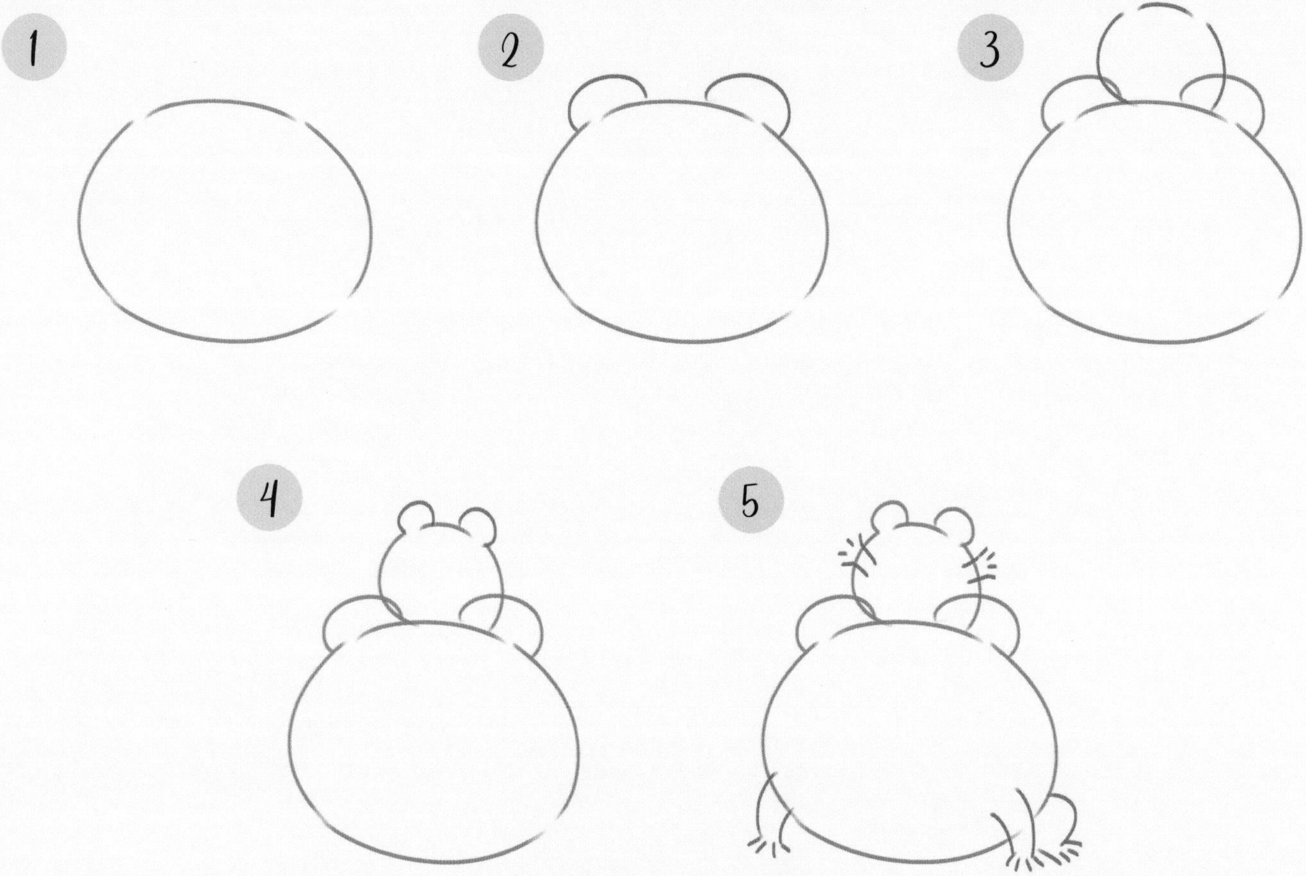
1
2
3
4
5

6

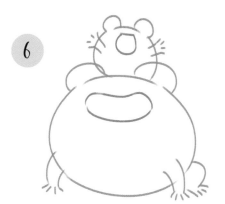

7

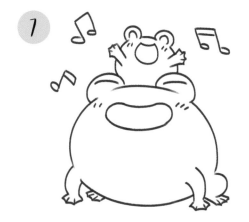

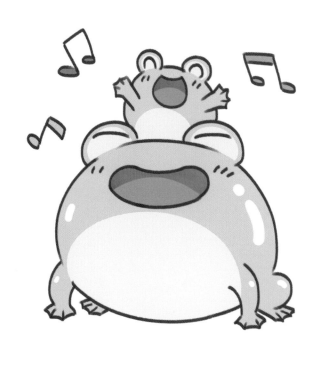

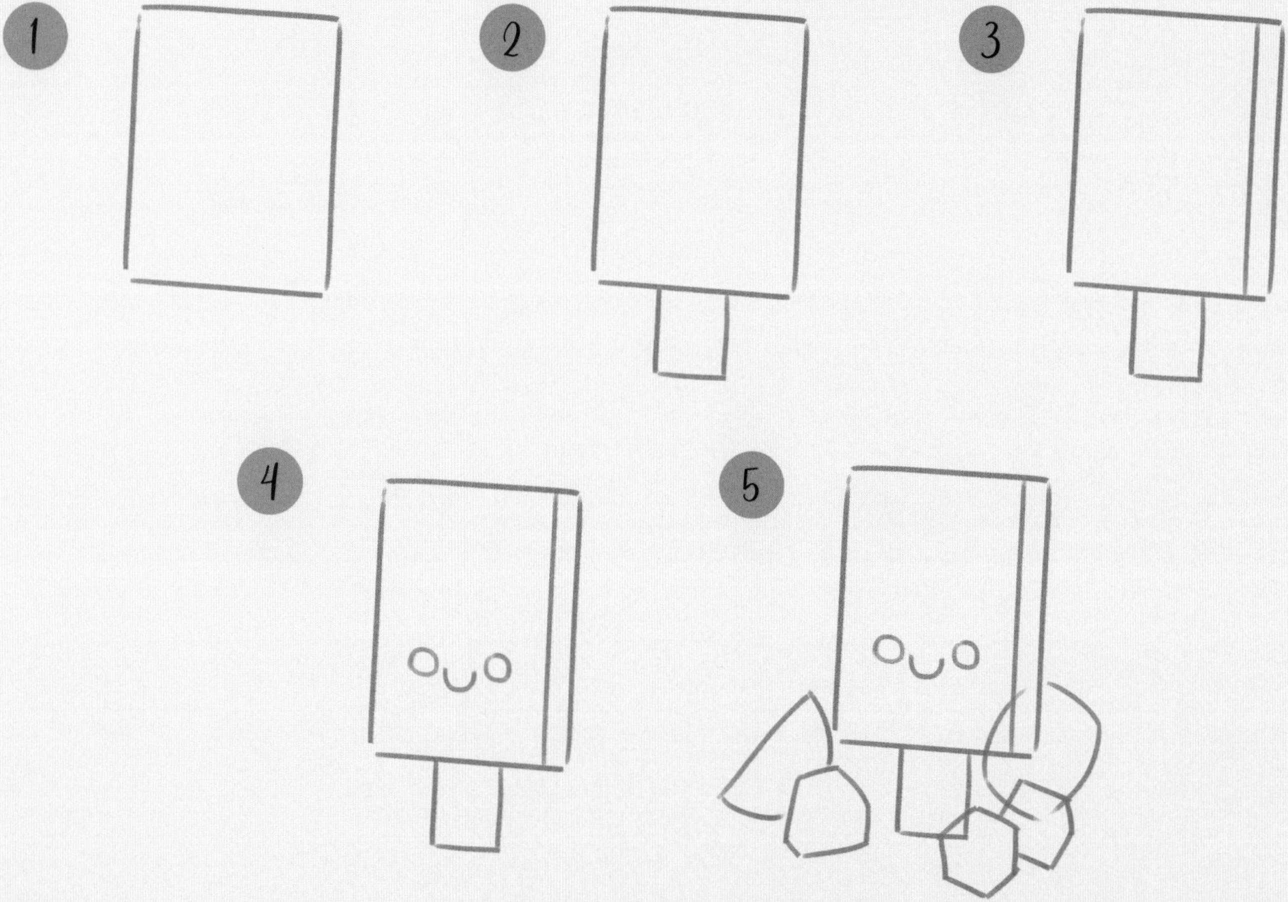
1
2
3
4
5

6

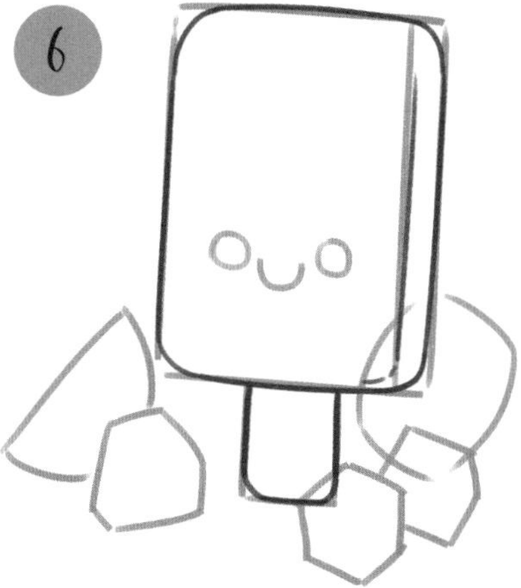

7

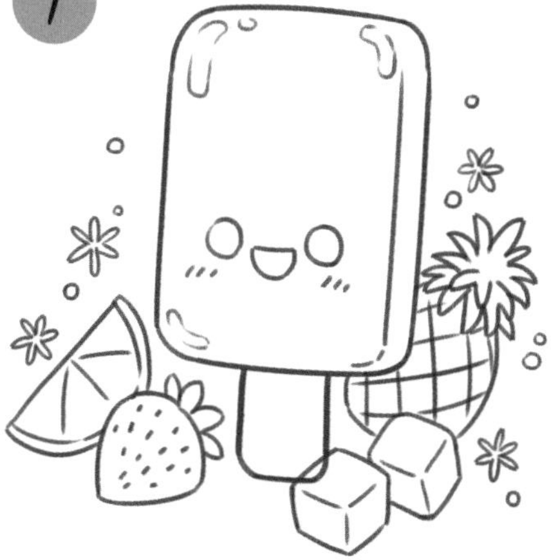

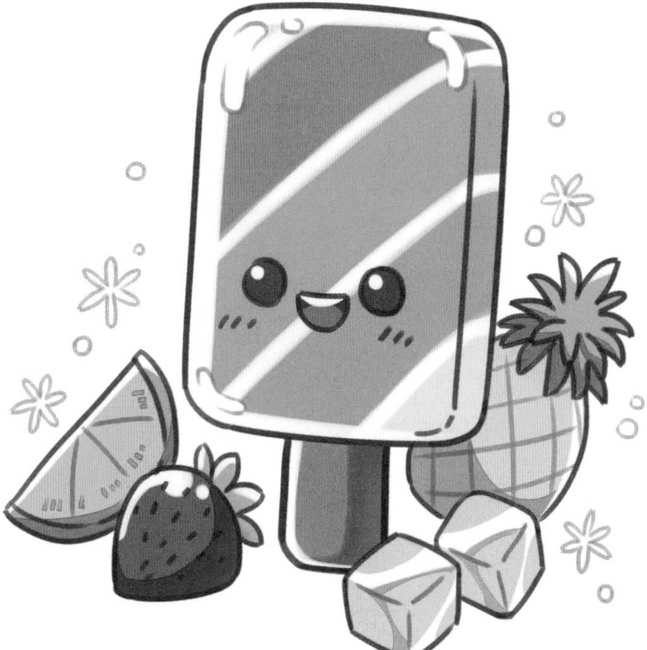

1

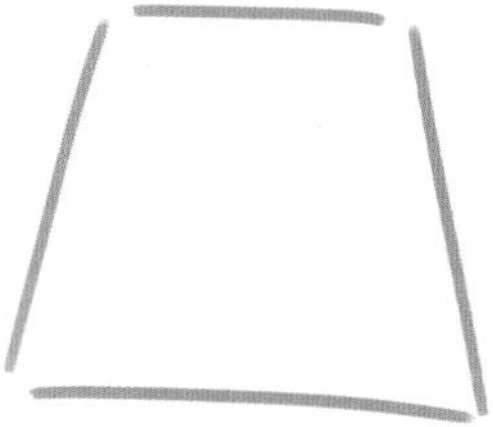

2

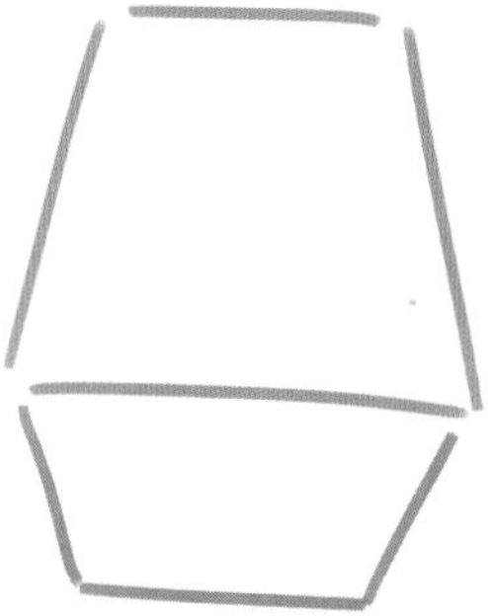

3

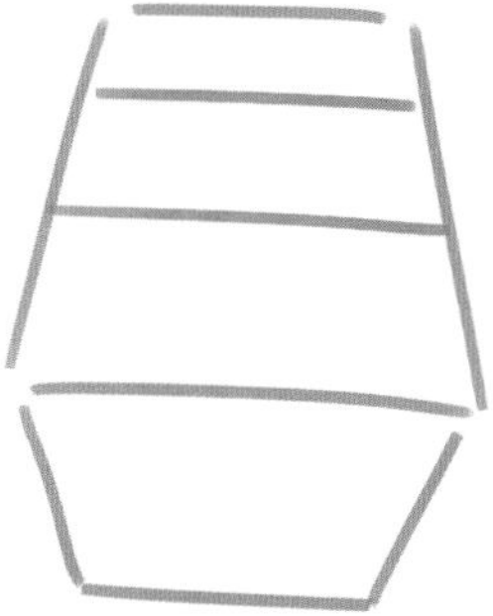

4

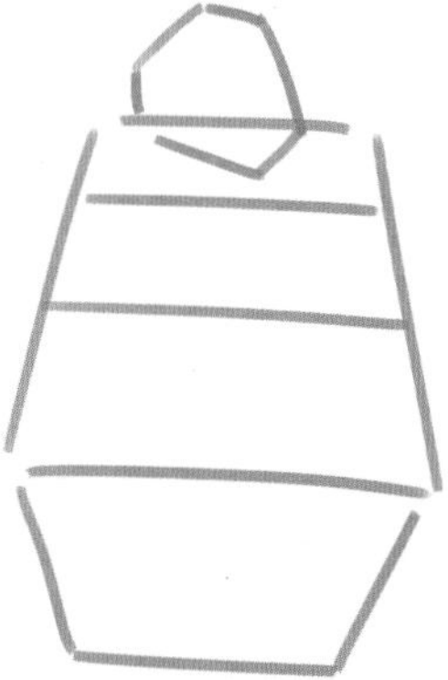

5

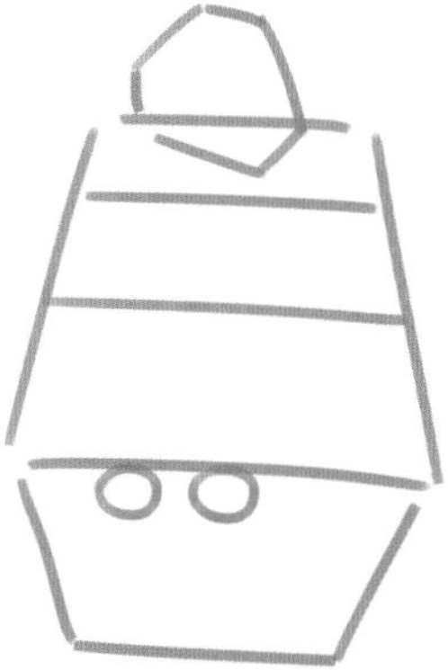

6

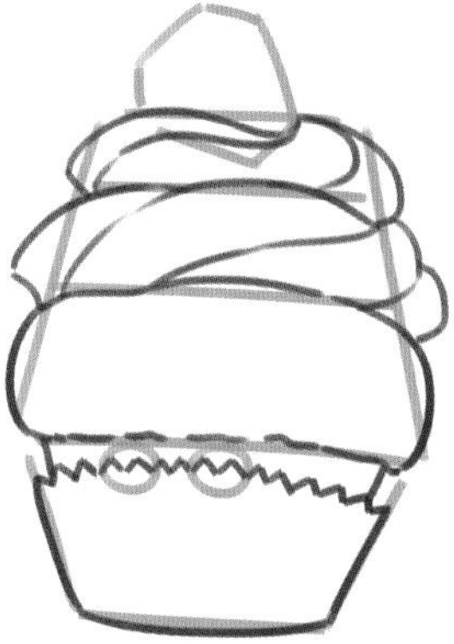

7

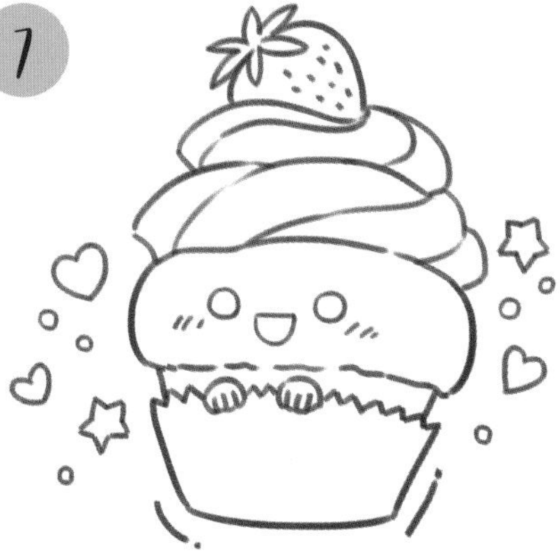

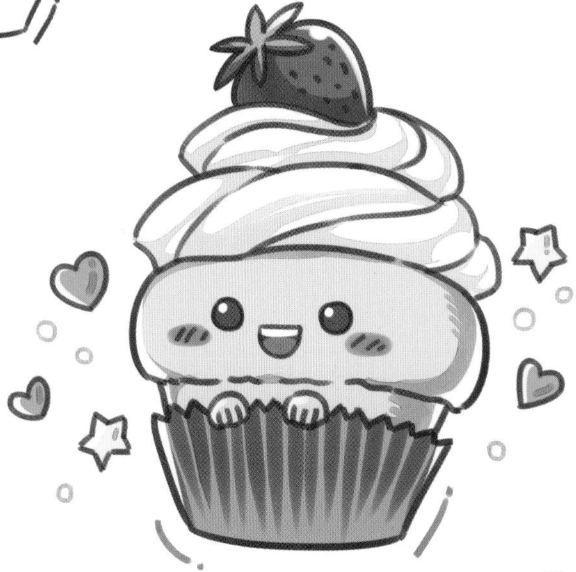

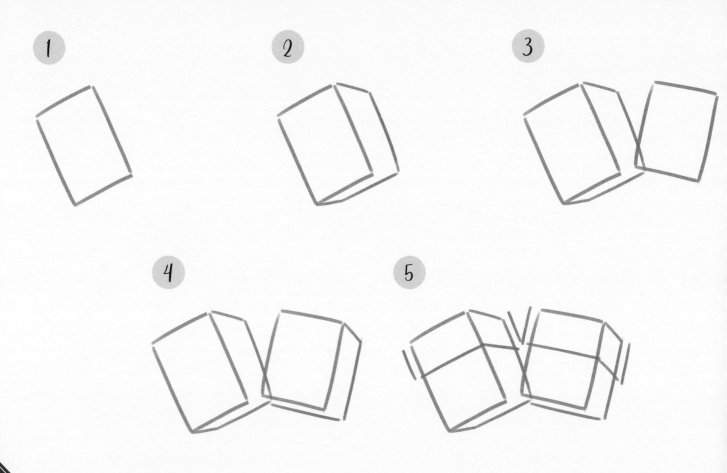

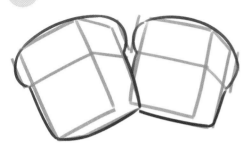

6

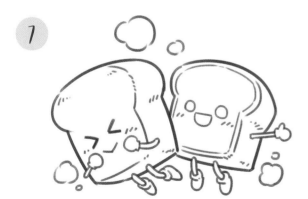

7

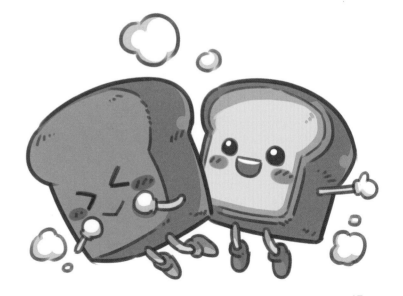

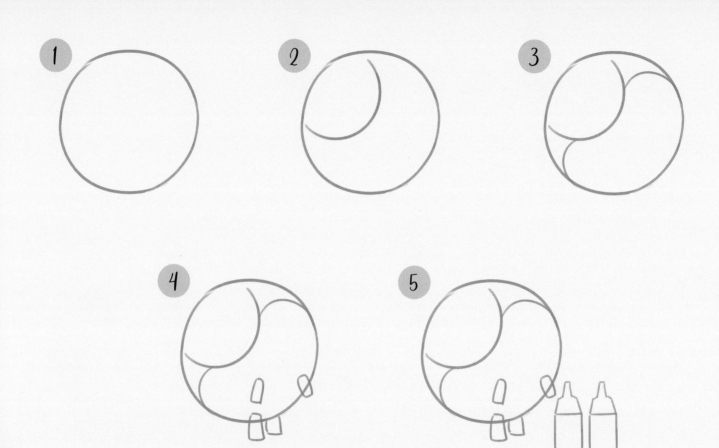

46

6

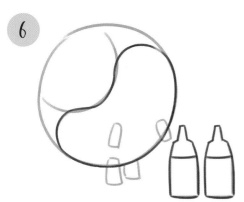

7

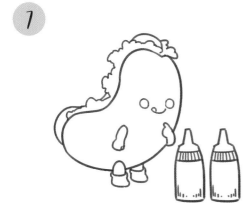

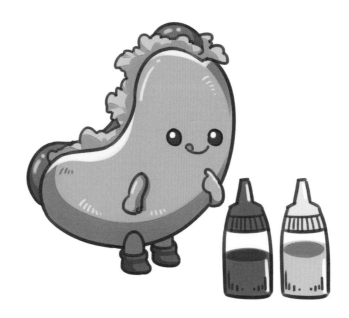

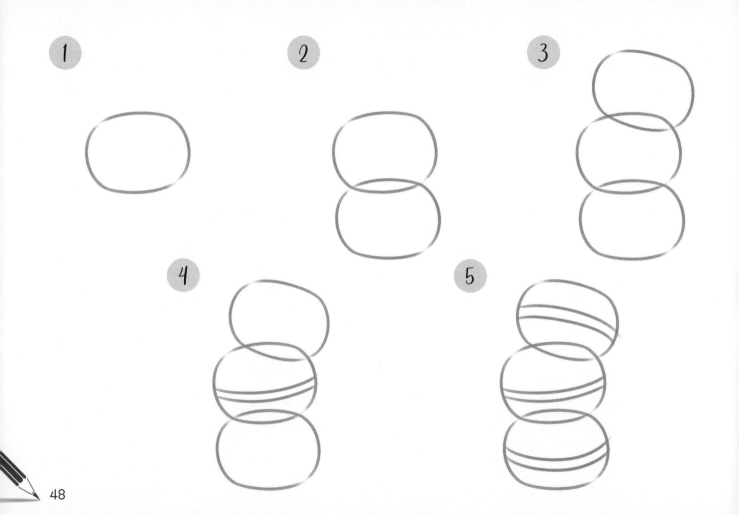

6

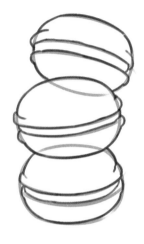

7

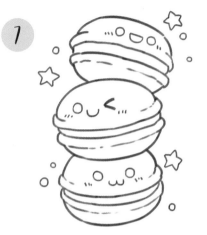

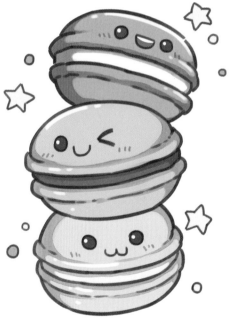

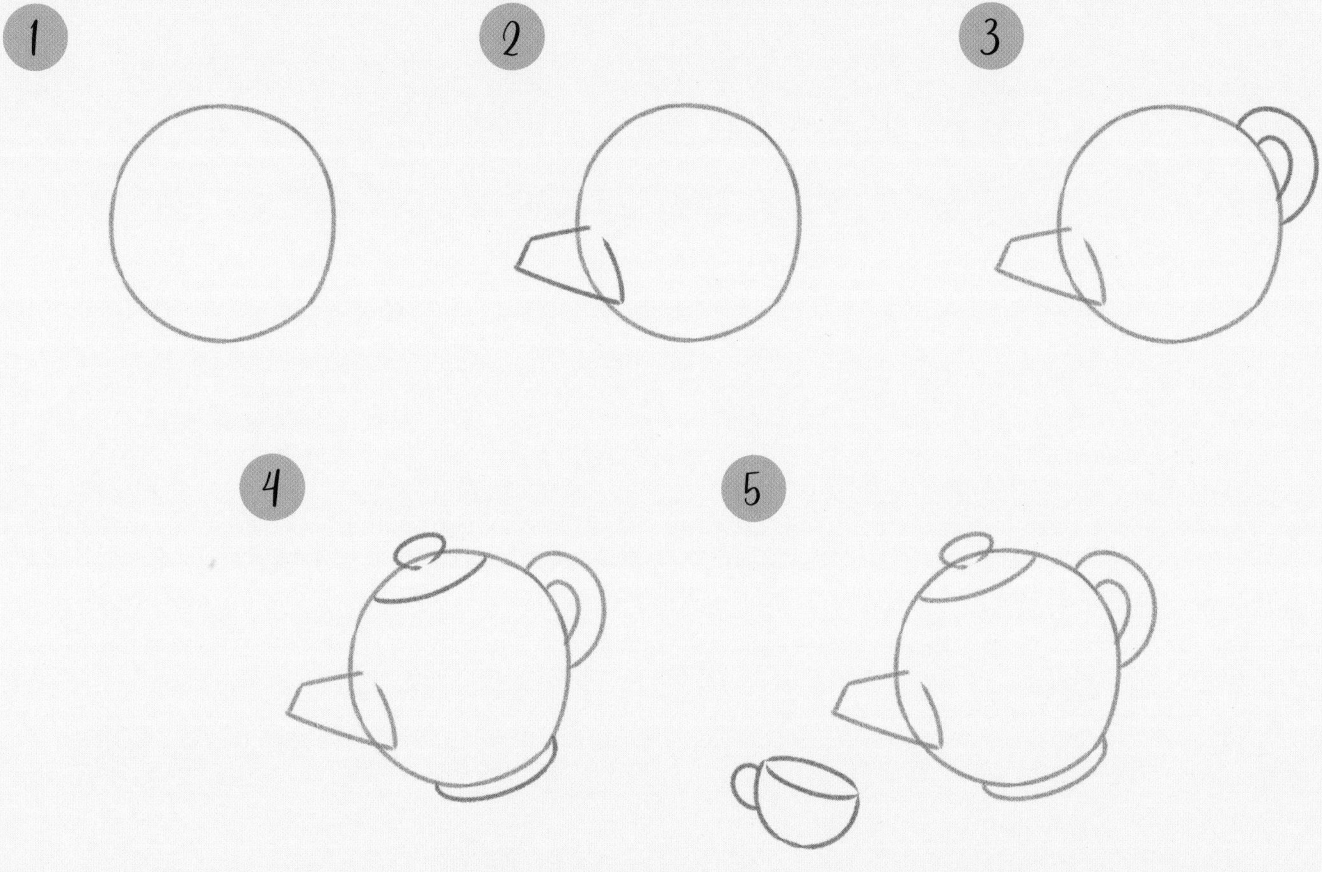
1
2
3
4
5

6

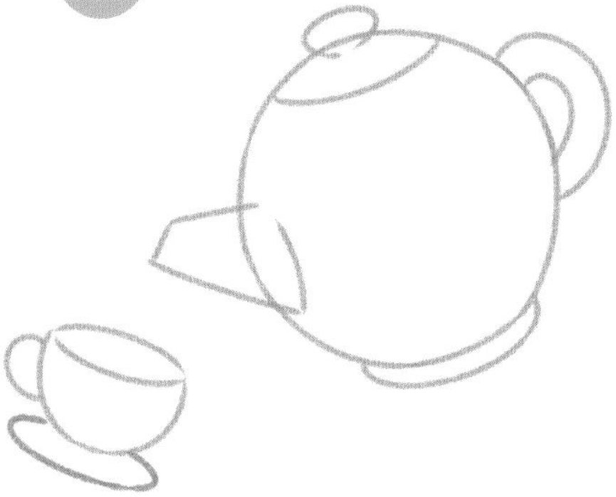

7

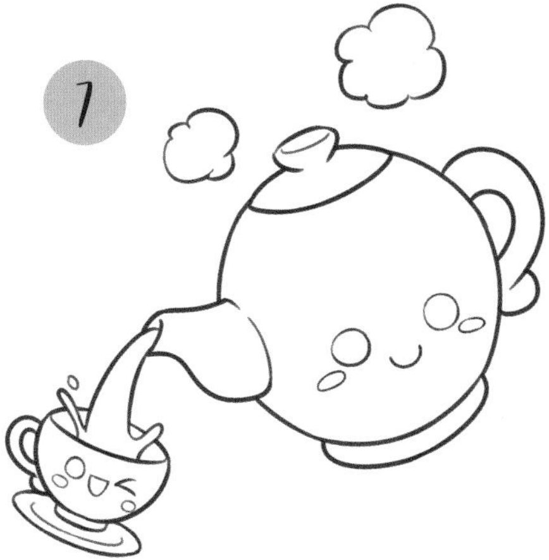

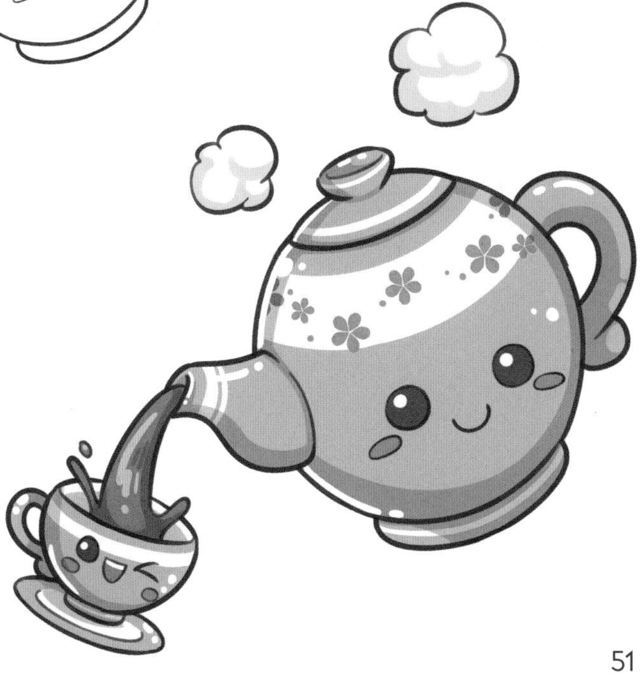

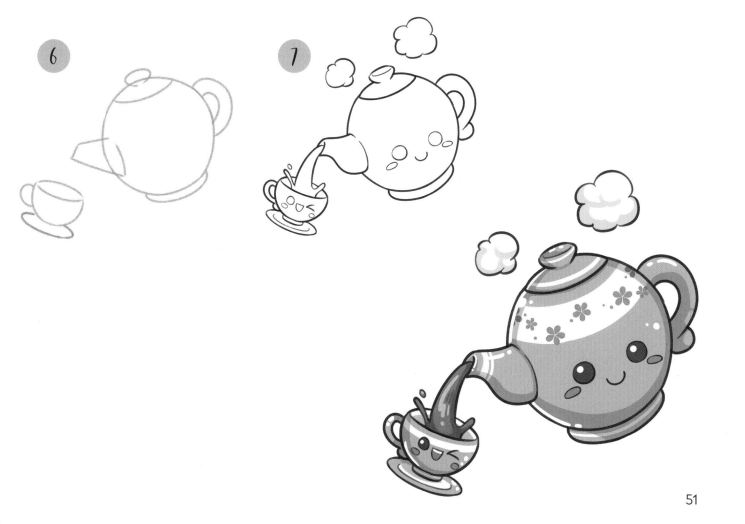

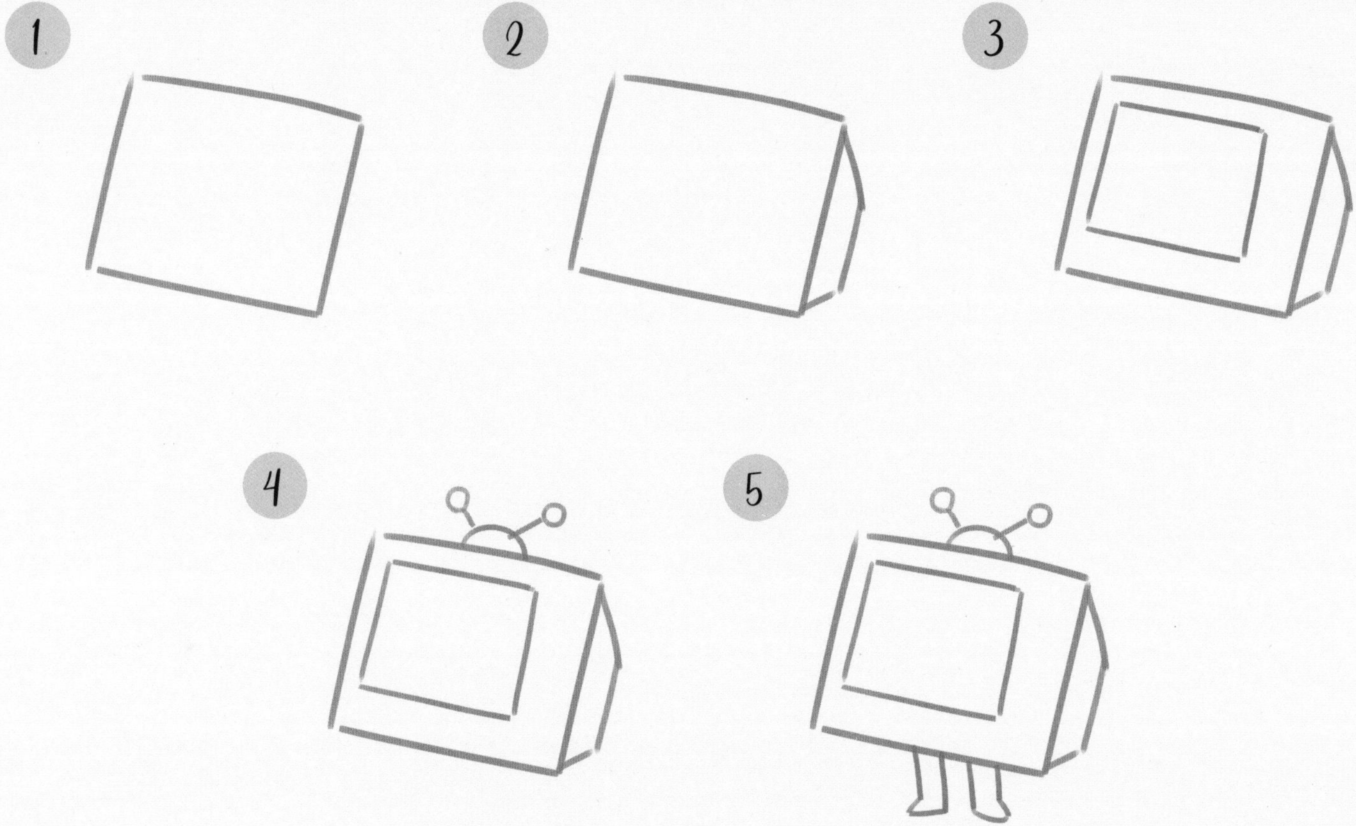
1
2
3
4
5

6

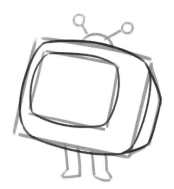

7

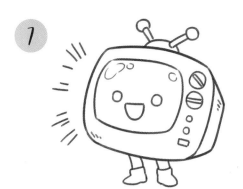

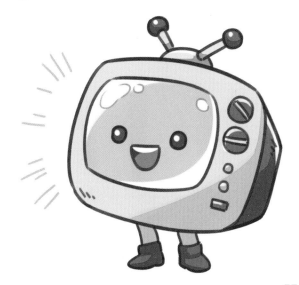

1

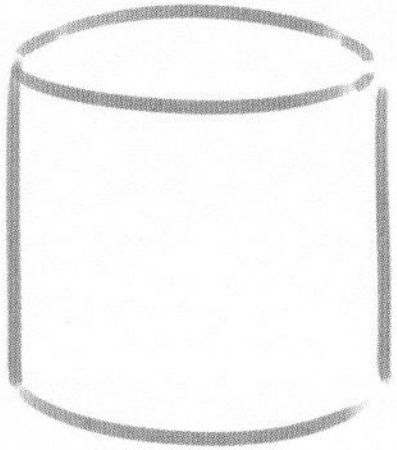

2

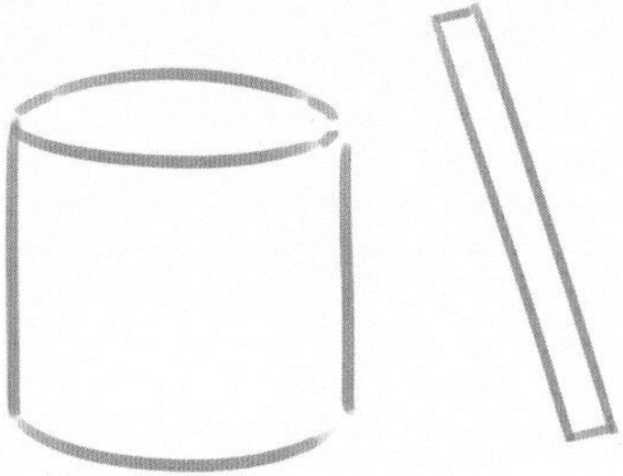

3

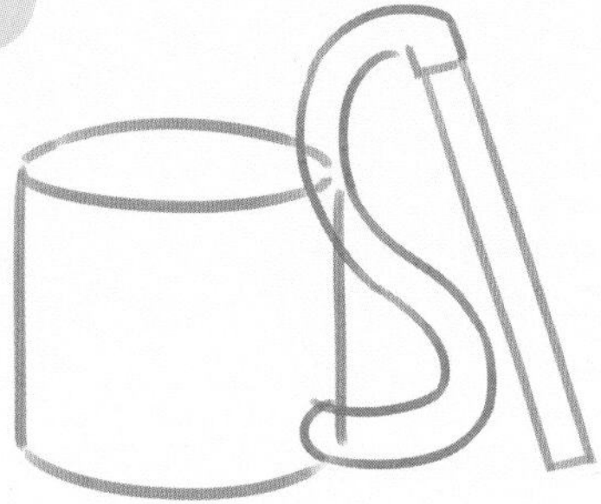

4

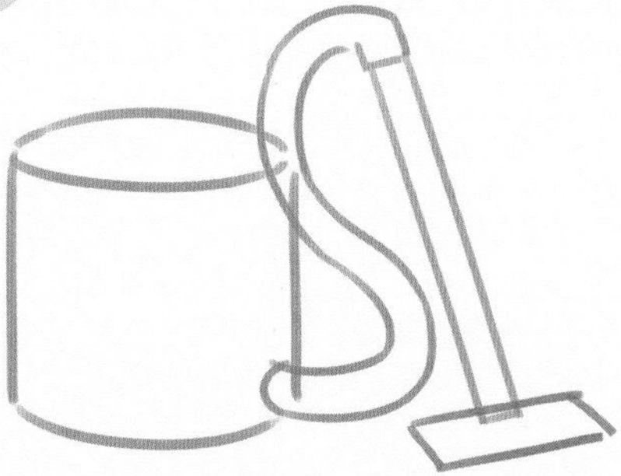

5

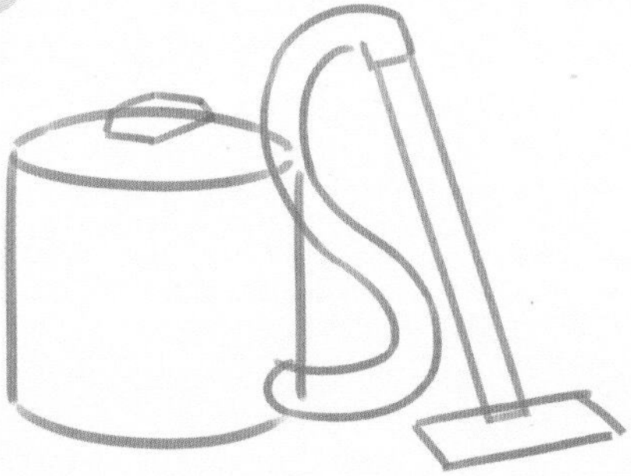

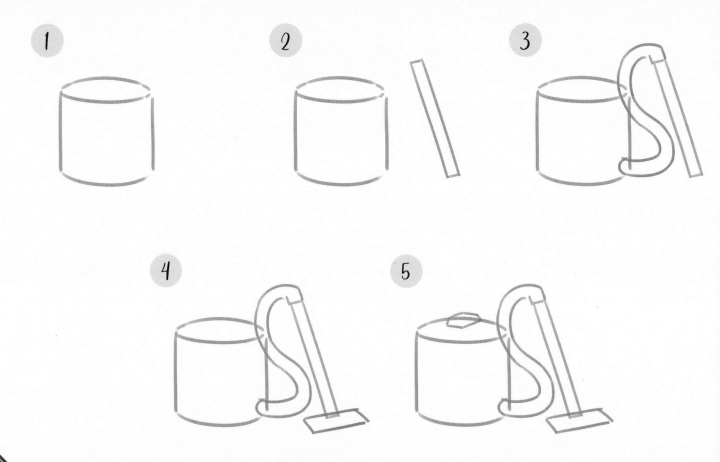

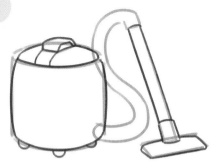

6

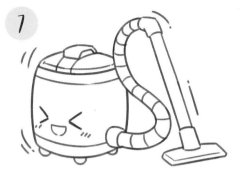

7

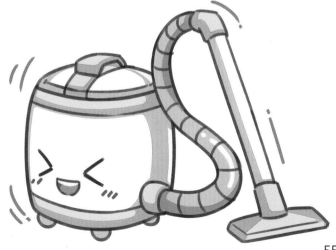

1

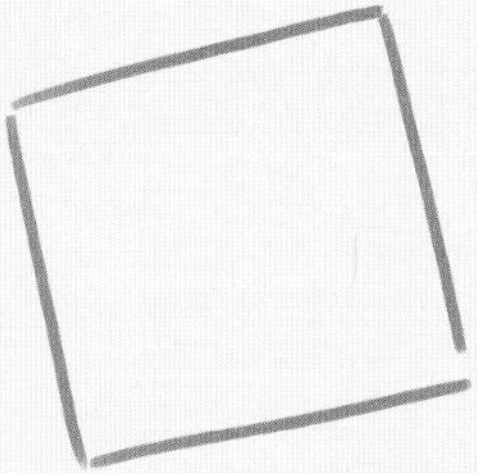

2

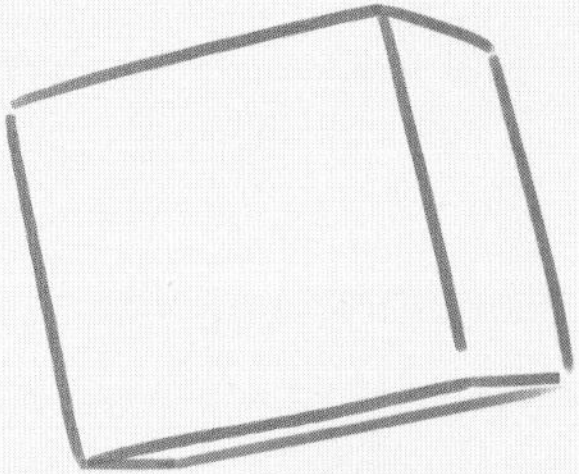

3

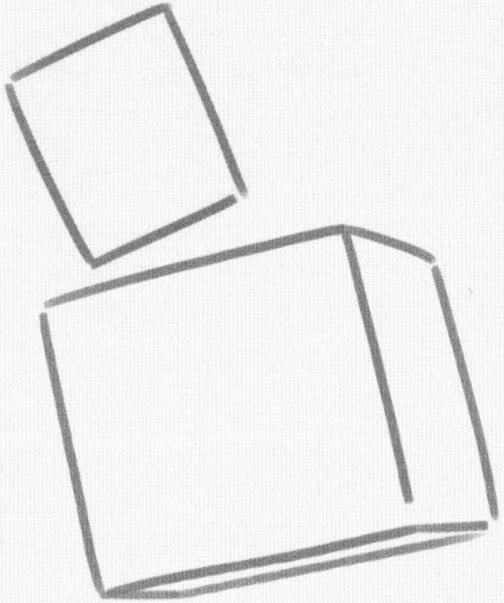

4

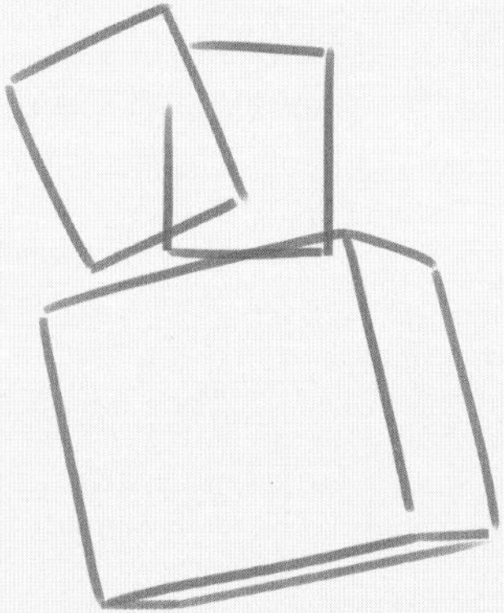

5

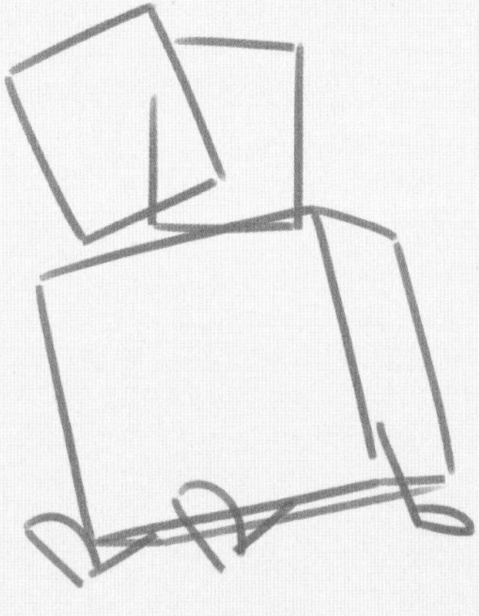

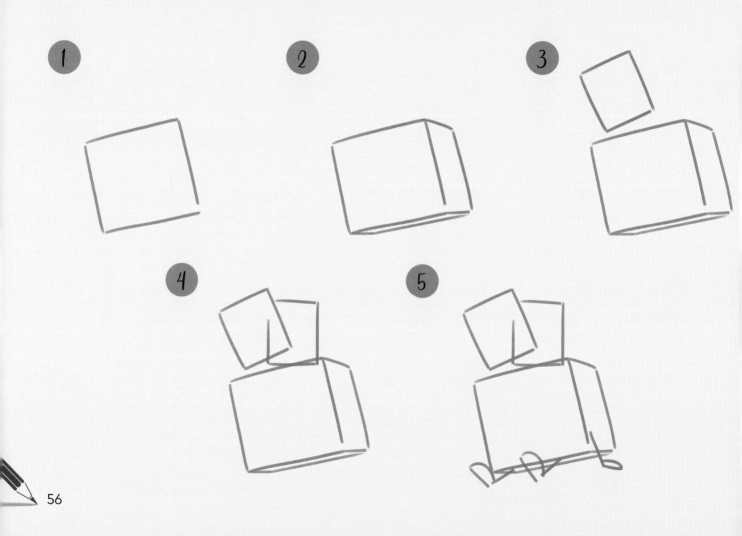

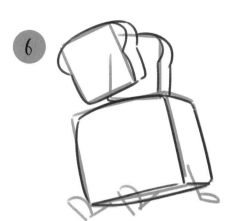

6

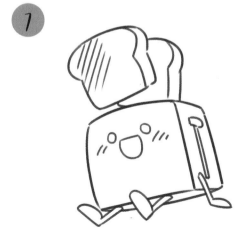

7

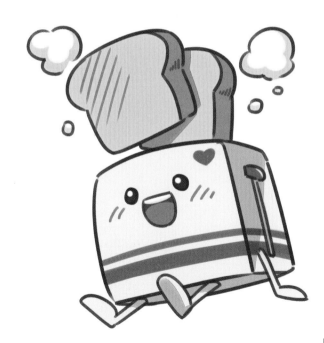

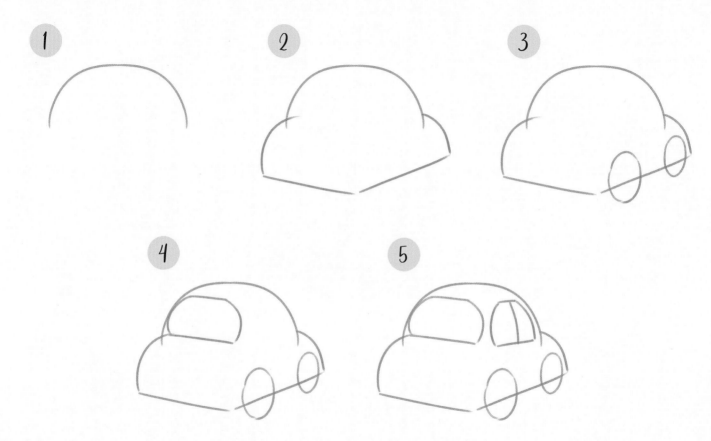

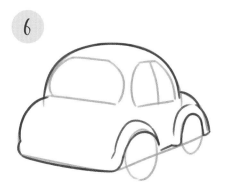

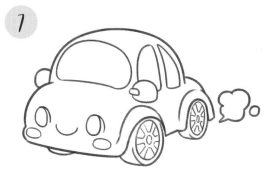

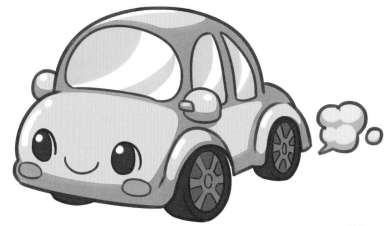

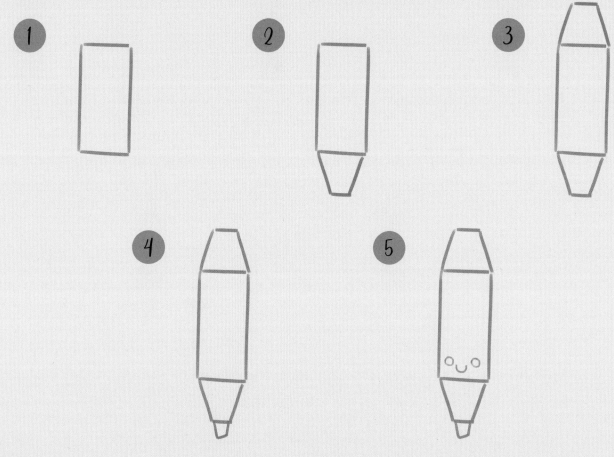

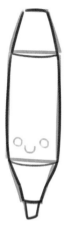

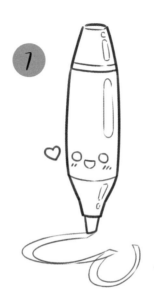

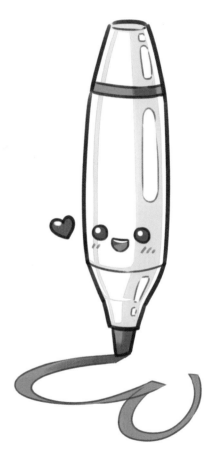

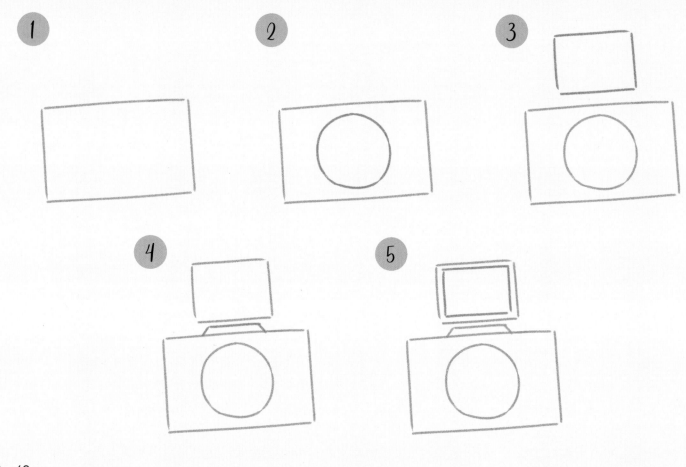

62

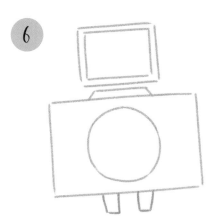

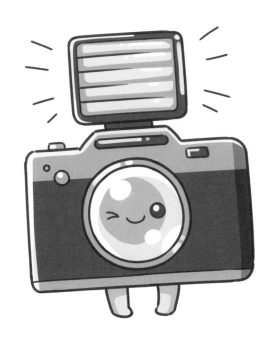

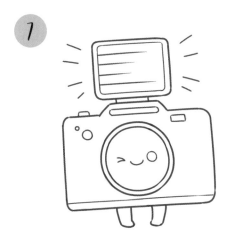

First published in 2023

This book uses material previously published in
How to Draw Kawaii, 2020

Search Press Limited
Wellwood, North Farm Road,
Tunbridge Wells, Kent TN2 3DR

ISBN: 978-1-80092-182-5
ebook ISBN: 978-1-80093-168-8

For further ideas and inspiration and to join our free online community, visit www.bookmarkedhub.com

FSC
www.fsc.org
MIX
Paper | Supporting responsible forestry
FSC® C016973

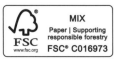

Dedication

To my daughter Amelia: you are the most Kawaii girl in the world.

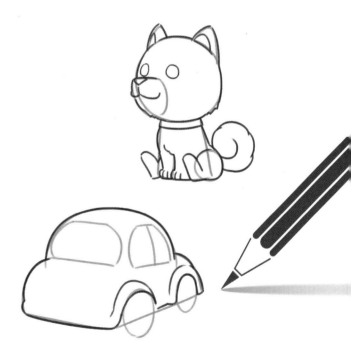

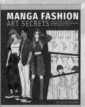
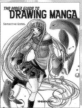
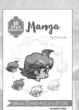
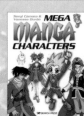
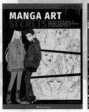
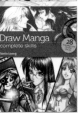
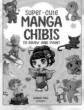

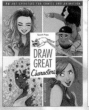
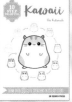

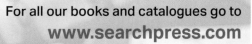
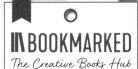